# THE WAYS
# TO NEW

# THE WAYS TO NEW

## 15 PATHS TO DISRUPTIVE INNOVATION

Jean-Marie Dru

WILEY

Published by John Wiley & Sons, Inc., Hoboken, New Jersey
Published simultaneously in Canada

*Library of Congress Cataloging-in-Publication Data:*

Dru, Jean-Marie, author.
   The ways to new : 15 paths to disruptive innovation / Jean-Marie Dru.
      pages cm
   Includes bibliographical references and index.
   ISBN 978-1-119-16797-6 (cloth); ISBN 978-1-119-21183-9 (ePDF);
ISBN 978-1-119-21182-2 (ePub)
      1. Creative ability in business. 2. Technological innovations. 3. New products.
4. Organizational change. 5. Strategic planning. I. Title.
   HD53.D78 2016
   658.4'063—dc23
                                                     2015029533

Printed in the United States of America

10  9  8  7  6  5  4  3  2  1

*To Marie-Virginie*

# Contents

# Foreword

If there is one phrase that I cannot stand today, it is "flat is the new up." Imagine setting yourself the target of drawing every game in a season. What a depressing mind-set.

Luckily, I have had the good fortune to surround myself with people who are dreamers, creators, and innovators. One man stands at the top of that field, Jean-Marie Dru, the original thinking man, who gave the business world the theory and practice of Disruption®.

Today and in the future some may find growth difficult. For extraordinary results one cannot take incremental steps. As Jean-Marie explains, "we must innovate in the way we innovate." In his new book titled *The Ways to New*, Jean-Marie has identified and detailed a series of paths that can lead companies to make a difference through innovation.

We are living in a world highly dependent on innovation. When President Xi Jinping was asked about what would be critical for the long-term future of China, he answered: "Innovation, innovation, innovation." In this context where innovation is increasingly decisive in the competition between companies, industries, and countries, it is key to use all available means in order to increase your success ratio.

True to the spirit of Disruption® that has been at the heart of our company for 25 years, you won't find a formula within this book that is the cure-all for discovering and creating innovation. There is no miracle process. Disruption® works through repetition, optimization, and approaching a problem with as much stimulus and inspiration at your side as possible.

Through a thorough exploration of some of today's most striking success stories, you can find new ways to inspire others to think differently about innovation.

This is what *The Ways to New* is all about. Enjoy.

—Troy Ruhanen
President and CEO, TBWA\Worldwide

# Introduction
# Why Marketing Should Drive Innovation

There was a time when marketing directors used to play a leading role in corporate hierarchies. That should never have changed. Because, quite simply, the role of marketing is to create growth. Organic growth: the only growth that really matters. Acquisitions may be strategic. But in the end, it is the growth of existing business that counts.

As a discipline, marketing has been through a difficult phase since the heady days of the eighties and nineties. Its importance has declined. People have grown wary of it. To such an extent that only a few years ago, marketing directors kept their jobs for barely two years on average. That can't be right.

According to management consultants Spencer Stuart, things have improved a bit. But many chief executive officers are still not entirely trusting of their chief marketing officers. That makes the latter's job harder. Even though that job consists of helping devise the company's overall strategy.

So a gap has formed between the importance of marketing, which is vital, and the way people see it. This is not healthy. Peter Drucker states the matter very plainly in his *The Practice of Management*, "Because the purpose of business is to create a customer, the business enterprise has two—and only two—basic functions: marketing and innovation. Marketing and innovation produce results: all the rest are costs."[1]

That tells us just how crucial marketing is. I would add that marketing and innovation should be seen as inseparable disciplines. The one strengthens the other. They are two sides of the same coin.

The Disruption® methodology makes them even more closely connected. Disruption® bridges the gap between marketing and innovation. On the one hand, it helps increase brand consistency and brand value. And on the other, it provides marketing teams with a tool, inasmuch as it gets them to see innovation as being an integral part of their job. This book is about this particular aspect of our method: how Disruption® can help marketing drive innovation.

The first part lays out the basic principles of our approach. The heart of the book lies in the second part, which describes fifteen paths to innovation. Any company, whatever its size, whatever the field, can use any of them to renew the way it innovates. The final part then reconsiders Disruption® as a whole and shows how Disruptive Brand Building can play an even larger part in the future.

(If you are only interested in case stories in disruptive innovation, go to Chapter 4.)

# PART

# ONE

# DISRUPTION AND INNOVATION

# 1

# Disruption and the Innovation Deficit

## The Innovation Deficit

Newspapers and business books have long focused on the digital revolution: on the start-up phenomenon, on the rise of nano-technology and biotechnology, on scientific breakthroughs such as in health care. Innovation, it seems, is everywhere. But the few truly innovative corporations that have come into existence hide the facts. People lump them together with the rest of the industry, over which they may cast a rosy halo. The truth is that many companies, especially those born before the digital revolution, are proving unable to innovate fast enough.

The problem is in the implementation. Research and development guidelines often seem too conventional. They limit rather than open up possibilities. Many companies are hostages to management systems, schemes, and procedures set in stone. You only need to look at the insufficiency of their organic growth.

A.G. Lafley, Procter & Gamble's former chief executive officer, has made a list of all the innovations launched by his company in the last decades, carefully distinguishing between incremental and disruptive innovation.[1] The latter are a minority but they generate more profit than incremental innovations do. Incremental innovations remain essential because they feed a continuous flow of new revenue streams, but they are insufficient, very insufficient. They do not ensure that a company will remain successful over the long term. Only disruptive innovation allows companies to stand the test of time.

Even Procter & Gamble, which ranks among the world's most innovative corporations historically, has only launched two truly disruptive innovations in recent years: Swiffer and Febreze. What about other companies? A 2011 report from Booz & Company[2] underlines that the two sectors most heavily invested in research, automobiles and health care, can boast almost no disruptive innovations at all (other than the electric car). The pharmaceutical industry is struggling to innovate. Fast-moving consumer goods companies are suffering from a lack of break-through products. As to high-tech industries, the story is obviously different. Their latest inventions constantly make the headlines. They are transforming the business world forever. Yet, they only account for 20 percent of industrial and commercial activity. They alone cannot compensate for the insufficient pace of innovation of business as a whole.

Every year, thousands of scientific articles report on some of the millions of patents registered around the world. But the proportion of these inventions that actually come to market is very low, no more than 5 percent according to official sources. And we seem incapable of increasing the rate of success. So a solution would be not to try and improve the percentage, but to increase the size of the sample: the cent in percent. In other words, we need a much wider base of ideas.

To do this, we will have to find new sources of inspiration. New doors need to be boldly opened. Different experiments and experiences need cross-fertilizing. A diversity of talents must be brought together. Intuition must be encouraged to speak. Bountiful encounters must lead to unexpected ways of thinking. This is the very essence of Disruption.

As Frans Johansson puts it in *The Medici Effect*, "Quantity of ideas leads to quality of ideas."[3]

## Disruption Methodology

The term *disruption* has become hackneyed. Twenty years ago, it was the term we found to define a methodology. Then the business world appropriated it and gradually changed its meaning. Today, people use the word *disruption* to describe start-ups offering lower product prices through new technology. And it is true that digital newcomers can often radically upset the market, constituting a serious threat to existing players.

However, I cannot agree with this definition of Disruption. It is too restrictive. I prefer our original sense. Disruption is not just a way of defining how start-ups clear the decks in any given sector. Disruption concerns all types of businesses, in the broader definition that we shall use in this book, at any rate. To us, Disruption® is a specific, three-step method: Convention, Vision, and Disruption.

Invariably, we start out by challenging existing conventions, ways of thinking and doing, based on preconceived ideas and deep-rooted habits. From there, we try to come up with a vision, a new way for a brand or company to define its future. And only then do we have Disruption, "the idea that will accelerate our journey from challenging convention on the one hand to renewed vision on the other."

From the earliest days, it became apparent that Disruption, in this sense, would prove relevant to advertising, marketing, business models, and even new product development. Think of it as a series of concentric circles: at the center sits the product; then comes the business model; and at the outer edges stand marketing and advertising. Electric cars are a disruptive innovation. iTunes is a disruptive business model, as are Amazon, Ikea, and Airbnb. I consider Southwest Airlines and The Body Shop to be marketing disruptions. And Old Spice and Red Bull are advertising disruptions. In other words, it is possible to be a "disrupter" at any level. The closer Disruption comes to the center of the circle, which is to say the business model or even the product, the stronger it will prove.

# 2

# Disrupt the Way You Innovate

We need to fight against the widely held view that Disruption is destruction.

Some think that our only choice lies between incremental, evolutionary strategies at one end and revolutionary but destructive strategies at the other. In truth, a whole range of strategies is available to us, so that corporations can improve market share by adopting a disruptive approach, without going so far as destroying their marketplace. Not everyone has to be Uber or Airbnb.

Having said that, many of today's marketing departments appear to satisfy themselves with only incremental innovation. They do what they can to make marginal improvements. But disruptive innovation, though more demanding of imagination and commitment, also always turns out to be more fruitful. Not only does disruptive innovation create top-line growth, it also has a powerful impact on the bottom line.


## Innovate against, Innovate for, Innovate with

So how does the Disruption methodology help? The answer is easy. It makes you think in many different ways.

Generally, most people innovate against or they innovate for. People innovate either where they think change is needed or because they believe they have something new to offer. In 1984, Apple innovated by challenging IBM. That was innovating "against." Sixteen years later, in 2000, Apple was no longer an outsider. It had become a global leader: it was bringing the fruits of its amazing inventiveness to the world. It was innovating "for."

Companies that sell fast-moving consumer goods tend to stick to "against" culture. High-tech firms tend to belong to "for" culture.

One interesting point is that the distinction between "against" and "for" matches the distinction between "Convention" and "Vision." This observation has given rise to two different innovation sessions in Disruption meetings, whether with clients or among ourselves. At the first session, "Innovating Against," we proceed according to the Disruption Method. In other words we identify market conventions. The aim is to dig up as many conventions as possible. Every one of them, however insignificant seeming, could turn out to be a launch pad for innovation.

The second session, called "Innovating For," focuses on choosing one out of a range of approaches to brand vision. These can be summed up, depending on the brand story, as "An Ambition," "A Belief," "A Mission," "A Viewpoint," "A Reason for Being" or "A Role." Every time someone comes up with a new way of looking at a brand, an avenue opens up for innovation. We also look at economic, cultural, technological, and social trends as well as dozens of related sub-trends. Then we take each one of these in turn and try to use them as a source of new ideas.

You can innovate "Against" or "For," but also "With." This is the subject of a third session, in which our goal is to think up partnerships, and more specifically unlikely partnerships between our clients and others. For instance, General Electric with Amazon or L'Oréal with Instagram. We devise imaginary and unnatural joint ventures—with competitors, customers, and suppliers, with traditional and digital retailers, with Internet players like Facebook or Twitter, with companies in the health care, energy, and education fields—three sectors in dire need of innovation.

I call such partnerships unlikely or unnatural, in that we feel free to include in our game companies whose activities are very different from our clients's. We force things in order to maximize creative tension.

## Innovate in All Shapes and Forms

Our fourth and last session is of another order. It is based on the fact that where innovation is concerned, most companies fail to venture beyond caution. Their methods tend to be repetitive, and not very inventive. We suggest that they look at how others go about things and study the way innovation happens elsewhere. And maybe get inspired by what they see.

This may seem simple, but it is important to choose examples after careful consideration. How many times have I heard our people tell clients they ought to act like Apple, say, or Nissan? This is a superficial approach that can lead to no serious rethinking and is thus useless.

Seeking inspiration from other industries or other companies demands hard work and insight. People need to understand exactly how and why their way of innovating is special. And thus grasp the key characteristic that defines their way of thinking and doing.

Bearing this requirement in mind, we have developed a tool that tells us by what means we can innovate: what the different types of Disruption may be. Here are some of them. Open Disruption, Asset-Led Disruption, Sustainability-Driven Disruption, Price-Led Disruption, Structural Disruption, Insight-Driven Disruption, Data-Based Disruption, Business-Model-Driven Disruption, and so on. We have divided these various types of Disruption into fifteen categories, which make up the fifteen chapters of Part Two of this book. We call these "Fifteen Paths to Innovation." Some are well established, others less so. Nearly all are digital-driven.

I will summarize our approach in three examples, each taken from case studies, to explain how it works.

Amazon is an instance of Asset-Led Disruption. When Jeff Bezos decided to become an entrepreneur, he started out by designing a highly original platform based on innovative information technology and logistical breakthroughs. Then he asked the question: to be most successful, on which playing field should we be competing? He came up with an answer: in the book trade. So Jeff Bezos did not start out analyzing market needs. He started out creating an amazing platform that became his main asset.

The Amazon example induced us to ask the following question: What if your core asset became the platform for innovation, rather than the products or services you sell?

Now that is a stimulating question. And the first in a long list this book will come up with. They can serve as a checklist before any meeting about innovation. (The whole list of forty-two What Ifs is in the back of the book.)

Toms, the shoe company, is an example of Disruption led by Corporate Social Responsibility (CSR). For every pair of shoes purchased, Toms gives an impoverished child a second pair. When consumers buy Toms products, they feel they are participating in a worthwhile cause. They show they care. CSR is at the core of Toms's business. It has underpinned the firm's success ever since it was founded in 2006.

This example provokes another question. What if you considered CSR not as a philanthropic initiative, but as a way to reinforce your core business?

Now the third example: Price-Led Disruption. To make its textbooks widely available to students and customizable by teachers, publisher Flat World Knowledge has put them on the Internet. Teachers can go onto the company's online platform and paste together passages from different textbooks at will to make up their own bespoke teaching tool, exactly suited to the course they are offering. Students too are allowed to buy just a few chapters at a time. No one, neither teachers nor students, ends up paying for something they don't need. Sometimes, the company even gives away a couple of chapters.

Hence the question: What if you decided to offer part of your products and services for free?

This book adopts a process based on induction. We take a specific case. The case leads to a broader question. That in turn can suggest strategies for a variety of products. Such approaches are mind-opening. They help shift the way companies think about their markets and about their business as a whole. In this way, the Disruption methodology helps them to rethink innovation. We try to open up new avenues for our clients by suggesting they ask themselves a whole range of different questions.

We encourage them to find those questions they never think to ask.

# 3

# Disruption in Practice

Disruption Methodology is a living organism that has been evolving ever since it was born. One day, in 2001, our Johannesburg agency took a radical step. It devised something called Disruption Days®. Within a few months, our entire network had followed suit. Disruption Days respect a precise schedule, with three or four exercises relating to each of the Convention, Vision, and Disruption steps. And each exercise has its matching What If questions. These run like a thread throughout every Disruption Day.

## Disruption Days

Internally, we use Disruption as a strategic planning tool. And we use it with our clients in the context of Disruption Days. We spend weeks, sometimes months, preparing for these Disruption Days. And, on the actual day, people from every department (marketing, sales, public relations, research, finance and human resources) at the client's company and of every rank meet our people, also from each of our departments and from every level of our agency. Usually, about forty people in all. We disrupt hierarchical structures. We avoid top-down habits.

So reckoning on three meetings a year (an absolute minimum) in each of our two hundred offices around the world, it becomes apparent that we have arranged more than five thousand Disruption Days. Perhaps as many as ten thousand. We do not keep track. And if you consider that some twenty people from each client company attend, then at least one hundred thousand people from our client firms have attended a Disruption Day. That is quite something. It shows that Disruption is indeed a key part of our culture. It is our basic asset. And our main competitive edge.

Designing a Disruption Day on innovation, we have decided to use the four sessions mentioned above, "Innovation Against" and "Innovation For" in the morning; "Innovation With" and "Innovation in All Shapes and Forms" in the afternoon.

A Disruption Day is a magnificent machine for making connections. It is a forum where everyone has a voice. I have always thought that pooling the imaginations of forty different people is worth a thousand individual imaginations. Now, if I were to say, "Come to a brainstorming session," you might think not much would come of this. And you would probably be right. A Disruption Day, however, is not a brainstorming session in the normal sense, because our methodology involves people working together toward a specific goal by way of specific steps. Again, having done Disruption Days more than five thousand times, we know what we are after.

## Disruption What Ifs

What If questions are so entrenched in the English-speaking world, in habits of speech and habits of thought, that some management consultancies have called themselves "What If" or used "What If" as a part of their name.

Twenty years ago, we didn't yet have recourse to What If questions to prompt innovation. We only used What If questions in the field of marketing. We had developed a process that involved giving clients a long list of What Ifs—thirty to be precise. Here's an example. What if we made a distinction between "source of business" and "the competition"? At the time, we had fallen into the habit of employing these two terms interchangeably.

I was then working for Le Printemps. This big Paris department store's direct competitor is another department store on the same sidewalk of the same boulevard, just next door, called Galeries Lafayette. But its source of business is actually the great number of fashion boutiques scattered throughout Paris. The distinction we established between source of business and competitor turns out to be relevant only in a very few instances. But when it is relevant, it throws up a really useful insight. In this instance, Le Printemps opened its floor space to a welter of designer boutiques. This was a great success. Galeries Lafayette followed suit. Now every major designer label has a corner in these two department stores.

Fifteen years later, Sony had us consider PlayStation. We asked ourselves that same question about the difference between "source of business" and "the competition." We realized that if PlayStation's competitors were Nintendo and Microsoft's Xbox, in reality, its source of business was Hollywood. Soon after, PlayStation games were designed according to the recipes that made blockbusters. PlayStation's campaigns were even made to look like trailers for Hollywood movies. The rest of the video-game industry did the same. Interestingly, for several years now, video-game turnover has exceeded the combined turnover of the movie business.

So a What If question we thought of in Paris for a department store proved relevant fifteen years later in Los Angeles for a video game console.

What If questions have become our methodological keystone. There are forty-two in this book. I described three of them already. (1) What if your core asset became the platform for innovation, rather than the products or services you sell? (2) What if you considered CSR not as a philanthropic initiative, but as a way to reinforce your core business? (3) What if you decided to offer part of your products and services for free?

These questions are thought-provoking, often intrusive, but at the same time, if you look at the whole run of them, they give an impression of being erratic, even incongruous and with no way of logic. And that is precisely why we have selected them. It is a sort of a "try and leave" model. Here is the way it works. We take the questions one by one, hoping one of them will prove inspiring. If the first one does not trigger anything, we move onto the next, and so on. It is very empirical. If only one of the questions inspires an innovation idea, then we know that the day has not been for nothing.

Brad Stone, senior writer for *Bloomberg Businessweek*, wrote in an article on Google X, "Absurdity is not a barrier to consideration."[1] That is true of our questions too. We like them to be provocative. We like them to be intrusive and even unsettling. And we like them to be unexpected, so that they provoke an intellectual reaction.

In his book *A More Beautiful Question*, reporter Warren Berger, who runs a website on innovation, considers the delicate art of asking the right questions. His study is based on an analysis of how creative brains think, how great innovators work. His the finding is that they all have a common denominator: endless questioning. Great products and companies are often born of a question. Today, he adds, too few companies encourage questioning, which should be the starting point of every innovation.

This is how, in his introduction, he defines what he calls a "beautiful question": "A beautiful question is an ambitious yet actionable question that can begin to shift the way we perceive or think about something—and that might serve as a catalyst to bring about change."[2]

Which is exactly how we work. Disruption embraces the notion of discontinuity. It shuns the step-by-step gradual processes that only seek marginal improvement. It is the opposite of what is behind that ugly word: incrementalism. We believe that steady steps do not provide real progress. We believe that growth comes from leaping forward by bounds.

And it is in that spirit that Disruption® can fuel the imagination when it comes to innovation.

# PART

# TWO

# DISRUPTIVE PATHS
# TO INNOVATION

**M**arketing can and must drive innovation.

To support marketing departments in their search for new ideas, we offer a framework for thinking. This comes as a series of different ways of innovating called "The Fifteen Innovation Paths." And this is what will be discussed in that second part.

Academic business writers have established many different forms of classification. Larry Keeley, for one, has identified *Ten Types of Innovation* (Wiley 2013) based on network, structure, process, performance, system, service, channel, brand, customer, and profit. In *Dealing with Darwin* (Portfolio 2008), Geoffrey A. Moore comes up with product leadership innovation, consumer intimacy innovation, operational excellence innovation, and category renewal innovation. The New York Academy of Science prefers to group modes of innovation into two broad categories: early linear model and convergence-sensitive model.

As far as I am concerned, not one of these different classifications is more relevant than any other. Not even ours. Each is the product of its author's own thinking. Each has a specific purpose. Our mode of classification is about collecting case studies into stimulating clusters, in order to come up with a range of thought-provoking questions.

Most business analysts see *disruption* as a term to explain or describe what is happening now in some industries or companies. Their approach is analytical. But to us, Disruption is not a theory: it is a method. It is not static: it is dynamic.

A theory defines and interprets what is. A method helps imagine what will be. It does not describe. It projects.

CHAPTER

# 4

# Open Disruption

"Our R&D department has grown from 7,500 people to something like 1.5 million, and we didn't raise our overheads," so says A.G. Lafley, Procter & Gamble's executive chairman.[1]

That quote is a tribute to "crowdsourcing," the path to innovation whereby a corporation opens up and exchanges ideas with millions of outsiders. Until recently, Procter & Gamble, one of the most secretive firms in the world, would never have considered taking such a step. It was obsessed with confidentiality.

When I was the account manager for Ariel, they sent unannounced inspectors to visit my office in Paris, to make sure that none of the company's paperwork lay loose on my desk. These impromptu visits were called "security checks." Today, Procter & Gamble works with a very wide range of outsiders, who may not be party to major secrets but are given information considered strictly confidential barely twenty years ago.

Wikipedia says Jeff Howe and Mark Robinson of *Wired* magazine conceptualized crowdsourcing in 2005.[2] Actually, collaborative innovation is much older than that. As early as 1991, Linux evolved a new way of generating software through open-source coproduction, democratizing innovation.

Twenty-five years later, crowdsourcing has become the business standard. Inconveniences, like the threat to intellectual property rights, have gradually come to be considered peripheral. Corporations have had no choice in the matter. Technology has become too complicated and the pace of change is too rapid. Survival means finding ways of drawing on outside resources and thus multiplying sources of inspiration.

Corporations now establish partnerships with customers, suppliers, and competitors; with universities, with non-profits, and all kinds of NGOs. They establish strong bonds with their consumers, especially "early adopters," who are livelier and quicker to react and know how to make their needs known.

They set up platforms to relate to customers: Dell Idea-Storm, Goldman Sachs SelectMinds, General Mills Worldwide Innovation Network (G-WIN), Solvay Innoplace, Nokia Ideas Project, CEMEX Suppliers Ideas Bank, Best Buy Customer-Centric, My Starbucks Idea. Lots of them. Down to "Riders of the Lost Ideas," NYSE Euronext's Program, designed to make sure good ideas don't vanish in a maze of red tape.

In future, applying collective intelligence will be the only way to find answers to critical issues such as "How Can We Use Shale Gas Without Polluting the Planet?" Or "How Can We Come Up With More Reliable Ways to Deliver Organs for Transplant?" Or "How Can We Deal With Water Shortages?" This last challenge will prove even more difficult than dealing with falling oil reserves.

History tells us every era devises the right solutions to meet the challenges it faces. Crowdsourcing is a solution to today's.

## Xiaomi: Design as You Build

In 2014, Xiaomi was ranked the third most innovative company in the world, after Google and Bloomberg. One of the reasons for this is that the leader in the Chinese mobile phone market is really good at listening. Large-scale crowdsourcing makes for infinitely more subtle listening ability.

Often accused of copying Apple, Xiaomi has in reality long passed that stage. It has become a really disruptive corporation. It is the current "Made in China" standards setter. Its business model, unlike Apple's or Samsung's, is built around software, not hardware sales. This means that Xiaomi can sell its smartphones at rock bottom prices, close to cost. The platform is open. Anyone with any other Android phone can download apps or content. This increases the number of users.

Handsets are available by Internet only. Customers recommend the brand over the Internet to those who do not know it. They actually become Xiaomi's sales force. The company remains on top of handset distribution, which it controls as it wishes. It often holds flash sales campaigns, with a limited number of products on offer. This avoids supply and stock management issues. In addition, sales events for new models inevitably create a stir. Potential purchasers are impatient to buy and this triggers a buzz in the media. All of which helps create an alternative and disruptive model.

Nonetheless, the real point lies elsewhere: Xiaomi launches "imperfect" smartphones, then offers improvements in stages over a period of years. In other words, it initially markets products you could call unfinished. This is because it regards consumer reception and reaction as crucial. Consumer reaction provides a foil for innovation, steering it in the right direction. Xiaomi calls this approach "design as you build." It is characterized by a very short time to market. Unlike other smartphone manufacturers, who launch a new product at approximately six-month intervals, Xiaomi offers a new model almost every week.

The corporation's product managers scrutinize user reactions on the Internet, showing an equal interest in complaints and in suggestions. No other company is so skillful at managing the digital ecosystem surrounding its products. Xiaomi is omnipresent on social networks. From forum comment to engineer's desk is only one short step. This makes for really quick reflexes. Certain products and services have been relaunched within one week.

The Xiaomi approach produces strong results. In 2013, the corporation sold 18.7 million smartphones. In 2014, more than three times the number. They hope to sell 100 million in 2015. Sales are showing exponential growth in China and India. A global launch is planned within the next two years. At the same time, the firm is planning to diversify into wearable technologies and home automation.

Xiaomi has turned "Made in China" into an asset.

## Lego: Co-created by Fans

While Xiaomi relies on customer response to improve its products as it goes along, Lego takes things further still. Its most enthusiastic customers—its fans—are also its product designers. The Danish corporation has actually made this a norm.

Inside a Lego Mindstorms box, as well as the famous little bricks, customers now find engines to drive the things they build. Within a few weeks of Mindstorms's launch, Lego found that its customers were inventing a whole range of new options by modifying the software provided. Lego had not anticipated that this would happen. But as hundreds of suggestions flooded in, they sat up and took an interest. Some thirty-five people offering the most promising designs were appointed official Lego "teachers," not employed by Lego but recognized as "trusted business partners."

One of them is architect Adam Reed Tucker, who came up with the idea for the Lego Architecture product line. They are replica kits of well-known real-world architectural landmarks. So you can now build a replica of the Taj Mahal, or the Empire State Building or Frank Lloyd Wright's buildings.

Thanks to its Lego Ideas crowdsourcing platform, the company can have its community vote for the best ideas. Those that received ten thousand votes—Lego is inundated with thousands of ideas—are then reviewed internally. So far, the platform has generated eight new models currently on the market. The consumers behind these ideas get 1 percent of the total net sales of the products.

Through its talents scattered all over the world, Lego finds awesome new paths for growth. It is working because the company understands that crowdsourcing is a give-and-take process. And this is why they share earnings and credits. Everybody wins.


## Procter & Gamble: A Cultural Shift

I know that Procter & Gamble is going through difficult times. But this should in no way affect our perception of the company's achievements in the long run. No other corporation has so influenced, shaped, and explored what is called marketing. As early as 2001, long before Web 2.0 happened, it set up an innovation platform called "Connect + Develop" (C+D). Basically, this was opencast lab work. P&G has become second to none in terms of organizing, implementing, and monitoring its global innovation network. It considers all new ideas, whatever the source. And this implies everyone in the company.

Connect + Develop has adopted a broader approach to establishing partnerships. It has developed relationships with thousands of high-tech companies, with Internet-based engines such as NineSigma (Procter & Gamble was in at the start of that one) and Innowave, a highly successful Eli Lilly spin-off. Also with private individuals, most especially retired people. As the latter constitutes a clearly underused source of creativity, Procter & Gamble set up YourEncore in 2003 in order to tap senior citizen expertise. Today, more than fifty companies, most of them Fortune 500 companies, have joined the platform. This entire synergy has been structured with great precision. As a result Connect + Develop remains the benchmark in open innovation.

In *The Game Changer*,[3] A.G. Lafley emphasizes that only 1 percent of the innovative ideas selected by Connect + Develop reach the market, which is not much of a ratio. It explains why Procter & Gamble has sought to broaden its initial portfolio to include every possible source of innovation (precisely what this book is about). The company's chairman has his own way of describing starter ideas and embryonic innovations. He calls them "fragile upfront ideas."[4] He wants everyone to catalyze everyone else's inventiveness. So that all the people in the Connect + Develop community feels capable of offering up an idea, however slender it may initially seem.

As to me, I see two other lessons to be learned through Connect + Develop. When crowdsourcing is arranged in a radical way, it creates both effectiveness and efficiency. Effectiveness first. Connect + Develop reduces time to market. Products that might have taken years to launch in other circumstances, such as the Oral-B Pulsonic toothbrush that Procter & Gamble co-developed with a Japanese partner, now come out within a few months. Efficiency next. Connect + Develop means that Procter & Gamble has to share some of its technologies with other companies, sometimes even with competitors. It turns out that, on the whole, competitors do not try to copy, rework or get around Procter & Gamble patents in their own labs. So in truth Connect + Develop partnerships help Procter & Gamble recover development costs faster. Fixed costs are amortized over greater volumes, generating significant economies of scale.

What goes for partnerships goes for acquisitions. These turn out to be all the more fertile when the objective is not just to mechanically increase turnover. The best-case scenario is when a target company's expertise helps improve purchaser products and services. So when Procter & Gamble bought Gillette, it was able to leverage know-how, often patented know-how, to the benefit of its historic product range.

The same applies to communities of innovators. Connect + Develop allows Procter & Gamble to enhance staff creativity. For example: the success of Olay Regenerist was rooted in the strange art of writing chemical formulas. A mere few years into its young life, the brand has achieved a several-hundred-million-dollar turnover. The starting point for all this was an unknown molecule proposed by a small, highly innovative French company named Sederma. Combining this molecule with other anti-aging ingredients identified by Procter & Gambler scientists is the key to Regenerist's effectiveness. Outside intellectual capital has reinforced inside creative force.

Connect + Develop has enabled Procter & Gamble to innovate faster. Five years after the community platform was launched, the proportion of new ideas reaching the group from outside intelligence rose from 15 percent to 50 percent.[5] It is still at that level today. Referring to Connect + Develop, A.G. Lafley recently said: "We literally opened the doors . . . Culturally, it was very difficult."[6]

All the new trends point to the vital importance of community collaboration in years to come. The Internet of Things and the Maker Movement herald a new industrial revolution.

Laser-cutters and 3D printers will turn us all into craftsmen, in the same way as today we all generate Internet content. This is going to revolutionize our everyday lives. The most successful companies will be those best able to fight back against new competitors born of these technologies. They may not be today's most competitive enterprises. They will be those companies most deeply committed to shared intelligence: those that would have been able to establish a knowledge-based community, with online co-creative capacity.

As Chris Anderson, who wrote *The Long Tail*,[7] emphasizes, these companies will redefine industry.

**Hence the questions:**

What if consumers were to become your own R&D department? Or your sales force?

What if you created from scratch an online community dedicated to innovation?

What if launching imperfect products were the best way to innovate?

CHAPTER

# 5

# Structural Disruption

*The Imitation Game* won four Oscars in February 2015. The movie is a biopic of mathematician and cryptographer Alan Turing, the Englishman who headed the team that succeeded in breaking the Enigma Code used by the Germans during World War II. At that stage in the war, the Germans were sinking up to fifty Atlantic supply ships every month. Historians suggest that Turing's team saved fourteen million lives by ending the war at least two years early. The devices Turing devised, known as Turing machines, are basically the first computers.

Turing's code-breaking team at Bletchley Park, near London, was inter-disciplinary. The word was not used at the time, but it well describes the way linguists, physicists, mathematicians, German-language experts, chess champions, and crossword champions had to work together, as well as of course cryptographers. Teams, like the Bletchley Park team, that bring together people of different talents stand a good chance of coming up with new ideas. Diversity and the confrontations it generates throw up new avenues of thought. Talking about Bletchley Park, Frans Johansson writes in *The Medici Effect*, "Diversity is a proven way to increase the randomness of concept combinations."[1] The book gets its title from the fact that the Italian Renaissance blossomed in the fifteenth century, when the Medici family gathered an incredible diversity of talents at its court, including painters, writers, sculptors, and engineers.

## Nissan: A Commitment to Transversality

Carlos Ghosn is passionate about diversity. Nissan was on the verge of bankruptcy when he was appointed CEO in 1999. Two years later, it was back in profit, with an operating margin of 10.8 percent.[2] This represents one of the most incredible turnarounds in corporate history. What was the key to Nissan's success? Well, obviously, there were several. But one outshines the rest. In *Shift*, his book about Nissan's recovery, Carlos Ghosn explains that as soon as he arrived, he set up nine cross-functional teams, relating to nine different priorities he had identified, among which were industrial platforms, dealerships, supplier relationships, logistics . . . [3] These nine teams included people of different nationalities, drawn from every department in the company. The head of the team in charge of manufacturing platforms would not be for instance an engineer, but a finance person. And the head of the team in charge of dealership issues would be a member of the legal department, not someone from sales.

Carlos Ghosn put those teams together in June 1999. He gave them three months to come up with recommendations, which then formed the basis for the famous Nissan Revival Plan. Sixteen years later, their recommendations still provide a framework for company thinking and for company work practices.

At that time, in the late nineties, I used to visit Tokyo five or six times a year. I saw Ghosn's cross-functional teams in action. They had to confront established hierarchies. This was all the more delicate, given that the team leaders were on average ten years younger than Nissan's heads of department. Building cross-functional teams was not a new technique in 1999, but it was not often used. Carlos Ghosn brought it into the limelight—six or seven years before words like "transverse," "horizontal," "collaborative," "community," and "transfunctional" became a standard part of every corporate head's vocabulary, in the 2.0 era.

## DARPA: The Limited Time Frame Imperative

One essential fact about the success of the Nissan Revival Plan was that Carlos Ghosn set a firm, really short deadline. Organizations that have almost nothing in common, like Google and the Pentagon, have made limited time frame a cardinal imperative. Chris Urmson, head of the self-driving car project at Google, promised Sergey Brin the car would be ready within five years, saying, "My son's nine. In seven years' time, he'll have his driver's license. I need to do better than that."[4]

Kaigham Gabriel, former head of the Pentagon's Defense Advanced Research Project Agency (DARPA) stresses the benefits of hard-to-meet deadlines.[5] They are why DARPA generates a high-volume flow of technological breakthroughs. *Harvard Business Review* has just published a list of them. There has been nothing else like it in the world of innovation. It includes the Internet, GPS global positioning satellites, stealth technology, and drones to name just a few. *Harvard Business Review* also emphasizes that DARPA is not expensive. It employs a limited number of people. Its budget is reasonably tight. As the review puts it, "With its unconventional approach, speed, and effectiveness, DARPA has created a 'special forces' model of innovation."[6]

If you ask people at DARPA why they are so unbelievably successful, they will underline the fact that their project teams live on an ad-hoc basis (the same is true of Nissan's cross-functional teams). "Each project has a fixed duration and a deadline. Leaders leave the agency when the project ends. This brings intensity to the projects and sharp focus. There is no such a thing as an open-ended project at DARPA."[7]

On a case-by-case basis, DARPA brings together the best people in the world, whatever the field. They may come out of industry. They may be academics. But there is no way DARPA could have hired even a few of these people on a permanent basis. Limited time frame is the key to making projects like these possible.

## Company Labs

DARPA is a self-standing organization, like a lot of the outside labs companies are setting up nowadays. This is done to avoid carrying the burden of traditional structures. R&D departments may be highly talented but they tend only to look to the gradual, the incremental. Company labs are there to create disruptive innovation.

There are so many of these labs around. Just to name a few: Google X, Microsoft Office Labs, Nest Labs, Foursquare Labs, Tesco Labs, Nike + Fuel Lab, MIT Media Lab. And that's not including hundreds of start-up labs. Our digital era demands quick reflexes. Labs rely on a transversal approach, short circuits, horizontal structuring, iterative thought processes. They are not after perfection, because that takes too much time. They work in a spirit of constant improvement. *Fail fast, learn fast* is their motto.

To learn faster, I would suggest that companies adopt the Coca-Cola model in advertising. Coca-Cola allots 70 percent of resources to established and successful programs. Then 20 percent is allotted to emerging trends that are starting to prove their worth. And 10 percent goes on new, untried ideas. This is the appropriate model in allocating resources for innovation: 70 percent on regular products, 20 percent on recent, breakthrough initiatives, and 10 percent on entirely new projects. In other words, 30 percent of resources should be attributed to disruptive innovation, which is what labs are for.

Labs are constantly on the lookout for talent, which is a rare commodity. And where talent is less rare, in Silicon Valley for instance, it is really hard to attract. But talent likes the way labs function. A Palo Alto TechCrunch contributor tells us why: "These shops are being set up similarly to fashion or game design studios, which is a great incentive to join."[8]

Labs are actually tapping into an old tradition. Remember how Thomas Edison set up an autonomous in-house lab within GE to explore the various things you could do with electricity. AT&T Bell Labs, where transistors were born, was in the same tradition, as was Xerox PARC, where personal computers came into existence (a huge source of inspiration to Steve Wozniak and Steve Jobs).

Airbnb was not devised by a hotel company. Uber was not designed by a transport company. Amazon was not set up by a publishing company. Netflix was not created by a cable company or a network. You have to believe that the world of established companies was not just geared to generating disruptive business models. To overcome a company's fear of becoming too rigid, a lab might be the answer. Labs incubate.

Labs are set up every day, and not just by tech companies. The entire world has been influenced by the "garage mentality" or the "Silicon Valley way" as it is called. Some businesses, founded long before the digital age, are setting up outposts on the West Coast. McDonald's has just opened an outfit in San Francisco, a way for the company to get " more plugged into the flow of ideas." People from PayPal, Microsoft, and Facebook have joined the new unit. L'Oréal, the French global cosmetics giant, has started a Connected Beauty Incubator in the same city. This is a lab with a mission: to develop connected beauty products. L'Oréal has already launched Makeup Genius, an app that turns your smartphone into an interactive mirror for a virtual makeup session. You can use it to try out a lipstick or a blusher on the picture of your face on your phone. This app won L'Oréal its listing in *Fast Company*'s 2015 "Most Innovative Companies" tally.

Digital Arts Network, TBWA's digital network, is structured as a set of labs, offering a single access point to more than a thousand digital experts spread across twenty or so labs on five continents. So we have, among others, social media labs, data labs, user experience labs, and e-commerce labs, in different cities. We even have a gaming lab in Helsinki. Every member of our network can access any one of these labs and work with it in real time. In other words: labs make for horizontality, creativity, and productivity.

## Salesforce: Innovation Catalyst

I was recently talking with Patrick Pelata, former managing director of Renault and now executive vice president of Salesforce. He told me how his company could help us make our labs even more innovative.

Salesforce's customer relationship management is well known. But what people do not always realize is how good the company is at making innovation happen. Having invented "software as service," which succeeded despite low sales in the wake of the Internet bubble collapse, Salesforce launched what was to become cloud computing. Marc Benioff, Salesforce's founder and CEO, is himself a brilliant innovator. He has found a way of matching the exponential growth in Internet capacity with corporate software requirements. He describes Salesforce as "a software company meets Amazon."[9] When he set up Chatter, an in-house discussion tool for companies, allowing people to publish in real time project-by-project progress reports, he described it as "a software company meets Facebook and Twitter."[10]

*Forbes* magazine has called Salesforce the most innovative company in the world for four consecutive years.[11] That is one reason for mentioning it. Another is that in cloud computing, its turnover is up with IBM's and Amazon Web Service's, four to six times higher than SAP's, Oracle's or Microsoft's.

Salesforce has come up with a genuine ecosystem not just for corporate management but for innovation as well. Without its various tools and platforms (Salesforce Success Community, AppExchange, Dreamforce Conferences, Community Cloud and Chatter, the in-house social media), radical innovations like PlayStation 4 and Microsoft Office 365 would not have hit the marketplace as fast as they did. Maybe they wouldn't have happened at all.

Shigeki Tomoyama, Toyota's managing director, freely admits that Salesforce plays a crucial part in delivering the Japanese carmaker's disruptive vision: "We want to create a new kind of car, almost like an iPhone on wheels."[12] Salesforce and its different platforms sit at the heart of that project.

Companies that want to speed up the pace of innovation where it is felt to be lacking need to fire on all cylinders. They need to use open innovation through crowdsourcing; they need to set up labs, with ambitious targets and limited time frames; and they also need—this is not optional—to draw on outside consulting services, crowdsourcing platforms like InnoCentive, innovation consultants like Ideo or IT solutions suppliers like Salesforce. Taken together, these will all increase the likelihood of innovation.

They will make it easier to meet the three challenges that are going to impact business in the next decade: the Maker Movement, Fab Labs, and Lean Management.

## Makers, Fab Labs, Lean Management

The first Makers event took place in Silicon Valley in 2006. Makers are do-it-yourself (DIY) fans who feel comfortable using laser-cutters and 3D printers. Much has been written about the Maker Movement. Basically, it is much easier for everyone to make their own products these days because of the improvement in rapid prototype tools. Thousands of entrepreneurs have come out of Maker culture. What they are doing is bridging the gap between DIY and industry. Soon, designing a "thing" will be as easy as setting up a website. The capital costs involved in manufacturing will not be a barrier to entry. The path from innovator to entrepreneur will be so short it will barely exist.

Manufacturing is about to become a cloud service. Every Maker, using a range of browsers, will have real-time and bespoke access to a fraction of the world's industrial infrastructure.

These days, Chris Anderson talks about "the long tail of things."[13] In his book *Makers*, he assesses the Maker Movement's economic potential. His view is that the fact we can all "change the world with an idea and an Internet connection"[14] is bound to transform manufacturing. The spectacular growth of digital business is spilling through into the real world. This is going to change industry beyond recognition and transform the world's economic engines. As he puts it, "The Maker Movement means you can be local and global, you can be a craftsman and an industrialist, low tech and high tech all at once . . . It means you can start out real small and become very big, very fast."[15]

Fab Labs are often spoken of in the same breath as the Maker Movement. They are a very promising way of generating new products. What Fab Labs do is speed up prototyping. MIT defines them in these terms: "A Fab Lab is a technical prototyping platform for innovation and invention, providing stimulus for local entrepreneurship. A Fab Lab is also a platform for learning and innovation: a place to play, to create, to learn, to mentor, to invent. To be a Fab Lab means connecting to a global community of learners, educators, technologists, researchers, makers, and innovators."[16]

Fab Labs are different from the labs we were talking about earlier because they are more open. Entrepreneurs, managers, artists, and do-it-yourself enthusiasts can come in and use digital manufacturing devices. Since these places rely on networks that distribute information globally, "an object can be designed," as one Wikipedia writer puts it, "in a Fab Lab, made in another and perfected in a third."[17] Collaborative structures such as these generate serendipity because the range of skills and expertise is so broad. They instill horizontal management structures and habits of cross-fertilization and transversality. They work according to a "creative commons" system, unlike many companies whose need to defend intellectual property remains an issue.

The Fab Lab concept has changed a lot since it first evolved in the late nineties at MIT, where they still have courses with names like "How to Make Almost Anything." Nowadays such labs don't have to be part of a university. They exist in industry too. Some companies like to develop their own in-house workshops. Others connect with like-minded firms in the same sector to set one up. Still others like to work with existing labs. Ford, for instance, has a relationship with TechShop, the first private-sector Fab Labs network, established in eight cities across the

U.S. and about to spread overseas. TechShop's goal, as its boss told *Contagious* magazine, is to "democratize access to the tools of innovation."[18]

TechShop has developed products as diverse as a high-speed electric motorbike, a James Bond–like jet backpack, a protective iPhone shell and Square, the payments system that uses the iPhone or iPad as a terminal. Since Ford employees have been hanging out at Detroit's TechShop, the number of new ideas at Ford in any given year has gone up by 30 percent, according to *Contagious* magazine.[19]

An International Association of Fab Labs, a network under the aegis of MIT, has identified nearly one thousand such labs around the world.[20] In June 2012, Barack Obama sent Congress a plan to boost the manufacturing industry. One of the measures proposed was to set up a national Fab Lab network open to all.[21] Some economists said this could in truth be a way of reinventing industrial manufacturing.

Ever since Chris Anderson published *Makers*,[22] people have been talking about the Maker Movement. Ever since Eric Ries published *The Lean Startup*,[23] people have been talking about "lean management." For a start-up to succeed, hundreds will fail. Venture capitalists and incubator managers know that too well. Which is why Eric Ries has devised a set of safety rules for start-ups. One of them is central to our purpose, because it relates specifically to innovation. The new concept is: "minimum viable product" (MVP). The idea is that rather than seek a prototype that is as perfect as possible, but takes too much time, it's better to inch forward in stages, by iteration. "You build a small piece of the idea, the piece that has the highest value for the customer," he says.[24] There follows a series of short cycles. Customer reactions make for a sharp learning curve. Gradually, the product improves. A bit like what Xiaomi does.

Or Zappos. When Nick Swinmurn started what has become the world's number one Internet shoe supplier, investors were skeptical. It has to be said that he just uploaded photos of standard retail-price shoes held in stock in traditional stores. A few easy, quick, cheap iterations later and Nick Swinmurn knew he had a potential market. In 2009, ten years later, Amazon bought Zappos for $1.2 billion. Collating customer feedback on unsatisfactory products and inadequate service ends up by improving innovation success ratios. This is what "lean start-up culture" teaches us. Companies are involved in a learning process. They educate themselves in almost real time.

The Maker Movement, Fab Labs, and Lean Management are interrelated. Time will tell whether they will have as much influence on business as people think. What we definitely know is that they are feeding a digital transformation of business that is opening up new opportunities.

Everything in this survey, from cross-functional teams to Fab Labs and Salesforce to Makers, tells us that innovation induces new management forms. Companies must become twin-speed vehicles. They need to have, on the one hand, research and development departments, and on the other, labs. Pure and applied research. Global and local innovation. Incremental and disruptive innovation. If they are to grow as much and as fast as needed, companies should have all these elements. They have to become what some business writers call ambidextrous. They must protect the present and get ready for the future. A company has to be prepared to reinvent its business model, but not at a cost to current business. There is no trade-off.

In order to get there, managers must show true leadership. They need to force through disruptive management systems. They need to impose uncomfortable methods. They need to adopt apparently contradictory processes. This can be tough. But as Steve Jobs put it, "Innovation distinguishes between a leader and a follower."[25]

**Hence the questions:**

What if you used the minimum viable product strategy?

What if you gave a limited time frame to all your innovation projects?

What if you created a lab or a Fab Lab?

## CHAPTER
# 6

# Asset-Based Disruption

Take inventory of what you are good at and extend out from your skills," Jeff Bezos once said.[1] He has definitely been following his own advice.

I certainly do not believe Jeff Bezos sat down in 1993 and thought, I'm going to start a virtual bookstore. The first thing he did was to devise a platform, combining top-of-the-line IT with breakthrough logistics. I imagine he then considered which sectors would suffer the most damage from the onslaught of this new infrastructure technology. Those that were the most vulnerable in terms of efficiency. He chose books because his platform was ideally suited to a highly fragmented market, characterized by massive stocks and small retailers.

## Amazon: The Power of Infrastructure

The "Earth's Biggest Bookstore,"[2] as claimed by Jeff Bezos, the very day of its opening, has proved to be an outstanding platform that evolves day after day. Building the capacity to take in millions of orders from millions of customers for hundreds of thousands of products, then source these products and ship them, involves investing huge sums. In the first ten years of its life, Amazon spent close to one billion dollars on infrastructure. And their top priority is to keep on building what will remain forever a core asset.

As Henry Chesbrough puts it in his bestseller *Open Innovation*, "Analysts thought of Amazon as a retailer. In fact, Amazon aspired to be a platform."[3] Well, it certainly is an enterprise with a vision: Jeff Bezos believes in open innovation. He opened his site to other merchants, making Amazon a retailing platform. He has even gone further, selling his know-how to other retailers who want the benefits of his expertise. Amazon also hosts third-party sites, becoming their infrastructure supplier. Now its expertise extends to data. The company has rolled out its first cloud computing service, allowing other companies to use it to build their own applications. In doing this, Amazon sells on its infrastructure.

"The best customer service," says Bezos, "is if the customer doesn't need to call you, doesn't need to talk to you. It just works."[4] Only immaculate technology gets you there. Infrastructure is both a core asset and a barrier of entry for the competition: a barrier to entry in which the company must keeps investing heavily.

So what is the real expertise of a company? What is its core asset, out of which the stream of products and services offered to customers flows? For Amazon, it is technology; it is the infrastructure. How about other companies? How about, for instance, Disney, DuPont or Apple?

# Disney, DuPont, Apple: Historical Assets

Fifteen years after the demise of Walt Disney, his eponymous company was in disarray. Its managers had ventured into businesses too far from the core. The corporation had lost its way.

In 1984, it was targeted by corporate raiders. A planned hostile takeover suggested selling off key assets such as the film library and prime real estate near the theme parks. As Todd Zenger wrote in the *Harvard Business Review*,[5] Disney's board faced a critical choice. They could either sell their corporation off to these raiders, who would tear it apart. Or they could fight back.

They decided to fight.

They convinced Michael Eisner to join the board. He pared Disney back to its main business. He resurrected Walt Disney's original creed, which was that the company's core asset is its studio: studio and talent made Disney the world's greatest animated film company. So Eisner refocused production on cartoons. His reward came with three giant hits: *The Little Mermaid*, *Beauty and the Beast*, and *The Lion King*.

Over the next decade, Disney's market share leapt from less than 5 percent to nearly 20 percent. Michael Eisner kept the diversified businesses: theme parks, stores, cruises, and Broadway shows. But he remained cautious. He made sure none of these ancillary businesses broke free from the studio. As Todd Zenger puts its, "Disney's broad array of entertainment assets draw value from a core of animation."[6]

You would not normally expect to mention Disney and DuPont in the same breath. Except that DuPont too underwent a period of poor sales before resurrecting itself through reemphasis on core activities.

DuPont has a long-standing record of technology-based innovations, including such disruptive breakthroughs as Lycra, Teflon, Kevlar, and Nylon. Eventually, though, organic growth through innovation started to decline.

One day, around the year 2000, DuPont management decided it was time to refocus on what had been the key to the company's success: science. From that moment on, resources were allocated to growth platforms in which DuPont's scientific know-how—both wide-ranging and highly specialized—was paramount. The company redefined its market space in simple terms: "Where DuPont puts science to work."[7] A slogan emphasized the new direction: "The Miracles of Science."[8] Today, DuPont makes one-third of its overall revenue from products launched within the last five years. And the interesting thing is that all of these products stem from refocusing on historic values.

Now Apple. Steve Jobs once said, "Most people make the mistake of thinking design is what it looks like. People think it's this veneer—that the designers are handed this box and told, 'Make it look good!' That's not what we think design is. It's not about just what it looks like and feels like. Design is how it works."[9] This is Apple's asset. The company is unbeatable in terms of "how-it-works" industrial design. No competitor has ever dared do what Apple does: package products without user's manuals. Only Apple products are intuitive enough for that. They bring simplicity to increasingly complex problems. Sir Jonathan Ive, Apple's chief design officer, is a big fan of Bauhaus-style minimalism. The quest for instant comprehension means removing every distraction between an object and what it is for.

James Vincent, who has been leading the Apple account at TBWA for more than a decade, speaks of "an art of reduction." For Apple, "how it works" industrial design has become the company's key asset.

## La Poste: Reinventing Oneself

In "Spirit of a Studio," "Miracles of Science," and "Art of Making," Disney, DuPont, and Apple possess core capabilities.

They may trace their origins back in time, but they are totally in sync with now.

But what if a company's core asset is not in sync with now? What if, unlike Disney, DuPont or Apple, a company's core asset is 100 percent tangible, and thus much harder to update?

This is the situation the U.S. Postal Service and the French Post Office (La Poste) have had to face. Each of these two organizations' core assets is a historic, coast-to-coast network of post offices, emblematic of former times. But unlike the U.S. Postal Service, whose capacity for change is severely limited by legal constraints, La Poste has been able to view this core asset in a new light, in order to offer customers new—and sometimes disruptive—services. Now its core asset is set to pivot.

Only a few years back, La Poste was one of France's most backward organizations. Today, it has started the process of turning its 17,000 sales points, its 90,000 mailmen and 140,000 mailboxes into a powerful new source of services. A very broad range of ideas are being tested in towns and villages throughout the land. French postmen will visit old or handicapped people daily on request. They will deliver medicine from drugstores to patients who are unable to come in themselves. Soon they will also be using smartphones to take certified photographs for insurance purposes. People will no longer need to wait until a claims expert has come by. Now La Poste is working on a smart mailbox offering access to local cultural programs and transportation timetables. People will also be able to use these mailboxes to place small ads.

In short, La Poste is transforming itself into a community-bonding device. One day, there may even be 3D printers in post offices, making every post office a neighborhood Fab Lab. The venerable old institution's list of prospective innovations is almost endless.

So, what can a company do that its competitors can't? This is the mind-opening question we always raise at strategy meetings.

It really resonates when you consider what Amazon, Disney, DuPont, Apple, and La Poste have achieved. Each has been able to build on a specific strength, a core asset, with long life expectancy and the power to generate a powerful bond between employees. That asset is bound to offer a unique catalyst for innovation.

As Thomas Jefferson once advised, "You do not have to be the best at what you do. It is better to be doing what others are not."

**Hence the questions:**

What if your core asset became the platform for innovation, rather than the products or services you sell?

What if you thought in terms of the things you do that other companies cannot?

What if you became a platform?

## CHAPTER

# 7

# Reverse Disruption

Around the year 2000, reporters and others started referring to Carlos Ghosn as "the Cost Killer." Well, he undeniably is a cost killer. But what he aims at goes far beyond just a mere cost reduction goal. His main concern is to add value. Cost savings are reinvested in the finished vehicle. And the same goes for productivity gains. So Nissan cars contain ever more equipment, have more efficient engines and better safety features. All for the same price.

## Jugaad: More for Less

It is hardly surprising to learn that the top adjective in Nissan's corporate glossary is the word *frugal*. Whenever I was in the elevator at Nissan Headquarters in Tokyo, I would always notice stickers posted left and right of the door that read BE FRUGAL.

Logically enough, Carlos Ghosn, an engineer by training, developed a concept called "frugal engineering."[1] This drew on a philosophy outlined in a book titled *Jugaad Innovation*, by three Indian analysts and prefaced by Ghosn himself. *Jugaad* is the Hindi word for "making do" or "finding a smart solution." The authors explain that in the developing world innovators are not after sophistication. They focus on whatever is "good enough."

Because we live in an age of diminishing resources, says Carlos Ghosn, "we must all do more with less."[2] In order to comply with this necessity, he decided to challenge the French and Japanese engineers on his staff to compete with Indians on their home ground of frugal innovation. He assigned the same engineering problem to each of the three different R&D units in France, Japan, and India. They all solved it. But the Indian solution cost one-fifth what the French and the Japanese came up with.

Suddenly, headquarters engineers at Nissan sat up and took notice of the way their Indian colleagues were working. They knew what the Indians were doing would prove relevant to Western European nations, where standards of living are now leveling out. Indeed, the Jugaad approach is not all that different to MVP or "minimum viable product," Silicon's Valley benchmark strategy.

Corporations in developing countries have to deal with non-existent infrastructure. They have to cope with deficient energy supplies, defective distribution networks, lawmakers, and bureaucracies that are largely out of their depth. Faced with all this, innovators must show ingenuity. Adversity foments creativity. Scarcity makes for inventiveness.

Jugaad is an Indian variety of what has come to be known around the world as "reverse innovation." Emerging nation researchers develop products specifically aimed at BOP—bottom of the pyramid—country needs. This is a broad category. It includes as many as four billion human beings. With these people in mind,

Nokia, for instance, devised the world's best-selling telephone, the Nokia 1100, a device designed for shantytown and dusty, low-income project residents, bedeviled by poor power supplies. It is robust. And minimal, with few functions. But it can be recharged within minutes. You can call someone. You can send texts.

Reverse innovation has developed a surprising standard. An 80/20 model: 80 percent of the functions for 20 percent of the price, compared to developed economy equivalents. The most famous instance of reverse innovation is a portable electrocardiograph developed by GE's Chinese subsidiary for its home market. In the end, some four thousand of these devices were exported. At first, Westerners bought them for emergency units, because examining patients at the site of an accident is cheaper and more effective than bringing the patient in. Then Western purchasers bought GE's cardiograph for hospitals too when they realized that most electrocardiograms do not need more sophisticated machines.

Counterintuitively, it turns out that reverse innovation does not lead to a lower grade of product. It leads to remixes that focus on what matters. Over a period of just a few years, these "redesigned" goods turn out to be increasingly attractive to developed economy markets. As Vijay Govindarajan and Chris Trimble say in *Reverse Innovation*, their standard text on the subject, "the future is far from home."[3] Renault's low-cost Logan vehicle, for instance, manufactured in Romania, attracts customers among both the wealthy and the less fortunate classes. In France, Paris's swanky sixteenth arrondissement dealerships sell the most.

## Lafarge: Local Labs Empowered

Indeed, reverse innovation may well turn out to be emerging market multinationals' secret weapon as they penetrate Western markets through truly disruptive innovation. GE chairman and CEO Jeff Immelt puts it this way: he knows what historic rivals like Siemens or Philips are going to hit him with, but when it comes to incursions of giant, emerging-market corporations into his territory, he is in the dark. Jeff Immelt runs one of the biggest companies on Wall Street and he is not mincing his words. He says it is going to be tough.

Western-corporation counterattacks will prove successful if they give their far-flung labs true autonomy. They need to stop wanting to centralize everything. They need to let local scientists choose their own priorities and decide what resources to allocate where. Too few companies do this.

But Lafarge, the world's largest cement manufacturer, does. It opened its first construction development lab in China in 2011. Then in 2013 it opened another in India. Both units are 100 percent in charge of their own investment programs. Some of their projects are not designed for our part of the world. For instance, a new cement-bonding agent that works on all kinds of different terrains. When mixed with soil—any soil—it allows Indian villagers to build homes that are solid enough to survive a monsoon.

But local labs have already reached another stage in "reverse innovation." They are generating projects that are not ever going to end up in their home markets. They sometimes respond to demands made by corporations or public sector enterprises in developed economies. For instance, Lafarge has come up with a solution to help fit cheap housing into difficult sites, where local constraints impede building. This applies to most of the historic city centers in Europe. The new product proved its worth in a small town in Southwest France: a concrete shell composed of different niches was demonstrated, in which houses and gardens could combine harmoniously on a variety of levels. Through this project, Lafarge tackled the thorny political issue of making affordable, green-conscious housing available to all.

The environmental crisis has obviously influenced what happens in developing countries. Lafarge's scientists and researchers around the world build ecological constraints into their thinking from the start. The only future they see is in sustainable construction. Consequently, what they do is relevant to developed markets too. Lafarge illustrates how strong a future reverse innovation has.

## L'Oréal: New Centers of Gravity

Naturally, to hundreds of millions of our contemporaries, who live in different latitudes than we do, and are only just beginning to enjoy the benefits of the consumer society, price will remain a significant issue.

Over time, though, the nature of innovation coming out of developing countries—those with the largest markets like China and India first—will come to matter more than price. The inventiveness and creativity of thousands of corporations in those two giant nations will prevail. It will arise from their capacity for bringing first-class technology to generate disruptive solutions to problems. Having said that, they are doing it already. Most reverse innovation is disruptive.

L'Oréal's research process epitomizes this new phase in reverse innovation. When one of the company's Asian labs finds a new molecule to help deal with wrinkles, the company can be sure this discovery will be useful in developing products for the world market, not just in Asia. This is what happened with Revitalift, a repair, anti-age, and anti-wrinkle product, which has become a worldwide success. Another example might be Elsève Total Repair 5, a L'Oréal's hair care product from Brazil where many people have the same specific hair problem. Now Total Repair 5 is Elsève brand's second-best-selling product around the world.

The center of gravity of innovation is shifting. Because the world is changing—and changing fast. A piece in *Harvard Business Review* points out that only ten years ago, when senior GE executives discussed world markets, they would refer to the United States, Europe, Japan and a place called the "Rest of the World." Sometimes it was just "The West" and "The Rest."

Now they talk about "resource-rich regions"[4] such as the Middle East, Brazil, Canada, Turkey or Russia and "people-rich regions"[5] such as China and India. Maybe someday, it might be the United States, Europe, and Japan that would be referred to as the "Rest of the World."

---

**Hence the questions:**

What if you did more with less?

What if you shifted resources to where the growth potential is?

What if you considered the 80/20 ratio (80 percent performance, 20 percent price)?

# 8

# Sustainability-Driven Disruption

We took 76 million Americans to the polls. More than in 2008 when Barack Obama was first elected. Our election was held on *refresheverything.com.* But what was it all about? The Pepsi Refresh Project, in which Internet users were asked to say what they felt about a range of charity projects put up by other users. Pepsi would fund the most popular.

Rarely had the Internet's full potential been used on so large a scale. A total of 183,000 ideas were submitted. This operation funded hostels for abandoned kids.[1] It renovated schools, theaters, and historic monuments. It helped build bike paths and playgrounds and basketball courts. It financed gyms and fitness centers. It put food into food banks and supported a whole range of charities, such as animal shelters and children's creativity schemes. It helped to combat illiteracy and lower school dropout rates.

Nearly all the projects became topics for documentaries. Many of the winners were interviewed. The films were shown on platforms like YouTube, which brought them—and Pepsi's innovative scheme—to a wide audience. This is a new possibility that will make everything different. Corporations can never again hold back on the grounds that any money they give away will not be noticed. No more claiming there is no real return on the corporate social responsibility (CSR) investment.

The potential offered by online information comes at precisely the same time that companies are really beginning to reason in terms of the triple bottom line. They know that their behavior will be judged according to three distinct criteria: economic, environmental, and social. Each of these aspects reinforces the next, provoking a virtuous circle. Respecting the environment and looking to the common good bring a shine to corporations, thus increasing their chances of commercial success.

In my last book,[2] published a few years ago, I was glad to quote the authors of *Firms of Endearment*,[3] who analyze the performance of thirty corporations, which, in their judgment, had showed purpose, including Best Buy, Whole Foods, Southwest Airlines, and Johnson & Johnson. These are all companies that refuse to make shareholder interest their main priority. Workforce, customer, and supplier welfare come first. The authors also insist on one other, essential, point. These corporations enjoy a higher profit ratio.

In other words, if a company is not just about profit, it will end up making more money. Staff turnover will be lower, productivity higher, the pressure on prices less significant and share price more resilient.

This book is about disruptive innovation; and this chapter is about CSR as a source of innovation. So I will not dwell on programs such as, for example, Unilever's remarkable "Sustainable Living Plan," which applies throughout the organization, from headquarters to the most far-flung subsidiary. As ambitious as this plan may be, which incites Unilever's staff to engage in social activities, it only occasionally stimulates innovation; this is not its objective.

I prefer to consider cases where solidarity leads to innovation.

For instance: our natural environment is littered with billions of plastic bottles that will not disappear for centuries. So Pepsi has chosen to put the full force of its brand behind *My Shelter Company*,[4] a nongovernmental organization dedicated to waste recycling. Especially bottles.

My Shelter Company's "A Liter of Light" project was first launched in the Philippines.[5] A plastic bottle filled with water and a drop of bleach (to prevent algae) becomes a lamp when installed in a roof, refracting sunlight. It illuminates homes for five to ten years and for next to nothing . . . In this way, the poorest of Manila's residents are able to economize electricity, which is particularly expensive in the Philippines. Furthermore, each bottle has reduced carbon gas emissions by more than thirty pounds annually. This initiative has permitted the creation of many jobs in the green technology sector. And last but not least, "A Liter of Light" is an open-source project, available to all. People can adapt it to their own circumstances.

Here again, "A Liter of Light" is another example of how limited resources and other severe constraints can catalyze creativity. And foster successful businesses.

## Toms: The One for One Concept

Philanthropy is a nineteenth-century term. It fell out of usage when a more comprehensive expression was needed to describe the sum total of what companies bring to society as a whole. People started referring to corporate social responsibility. But firms like Ben & Jerry's, thirty years ago, pioneered a return to the idea of corporate philanthropy. Today, "One for One" has become the epitome of new-style corporate philanthropy. No firm embodies this better than Toms. As it has already been said, whenever Toms sells a pair of shoes, it donates another pair to a child in need. Toms founder, Blake Mycoskie, is upfront about this. "Giving," he says, "helps generate revenue."[6]

As a concept, "One for One" is very powerful. Mycoskie is extending it gradually to other sectors. The horizontality of his diversification has nothing to do with classic strategies based on technological or commercial adjacency between current and future activities. As far as he is concerned, the brand is the starting point. The brand and what it means to customers.

Toms has been involved in other businesses besides shoes, but none has come to matter as much as its most recent venture, into coffee. Every package of beans sold will buy someone in a supplier country—Guatemala, Honduras, Peru, or Rwanda— clean water for a week. As with the shoe scheme, an outside partner has been found to handle water distribution in association with Toms coffee-trading subsidiary, Toms Roasting Co.: in this instance, an international charity named Water for People. The whole operation is summed up by the slogan "Coffee for You, Water for All."

Mycoskie wants to extend his "One for One" idea to other sectors. At least ten, if press reports are to be believed.[7] If you are worried he may not be able to go on replicating his shoe success across the board, you need to listen to what Richard Branson had to say about Toms's chief executive. Branson is the man who brilliantly applied his "anti-establishment" logic to a whole raft of different sectors from music to aviation via financial services, the media, and even a wedding-gown business. He told *Fortune* magazine, "In fact, if you're too smarty-pants, and every single thing you do is successful, in some ways the public isn't as endeared to you as if you sometimes fall flat on your face."[8]

Mycoskie represents a new generation of corporate chiefs who believe keeping business and social responsibility apart makes no sense. In a nutshell, he says, "What does the world need? And how can we address it with a commercial endeavor?"[9]

## Philips: Much More than Better Light

Philips has been selling light for some 120 years. The only thing anyone ever asked of a light bulb is that it would work. Period. Then Philips became a pioneer in the development of light-emitting diodes, better known as LEDs. It is currently world leader in the field.

At the outset, Philips executives were faced with a huge dilemma. Should they invest massively in LED technology? Or do everything they could to stop a burgeoning market that was going to dramatically decrease sales of their products? Light-emitting diodes last more than 20 years, five or six times longer than standard bulbs.

In the end, senior executives decided to undermine their own sales. As Fast Company's editor-at-large, Jon Gertner, explains in an article, the basic thinking was social responsibility. Backing LED technology meant backing sustainability. LEDs use 15 percent of the power standard light bulbs use to achieve the same luminosity. Over 20 years, in the United States alone, that difference represents a saving of some $250 billion.

I do not know if Philips will continue with the LED business. As I review these lines before printing, *The Wall Street Journal* reported on rumors that the company has shed its lighting components division to focus on its medical equipment and lifestyle products. This may, at first sight, make this Philips example appear less compelling. But it should not however draw a veil over the company's strong, crucial contribution to the sustainable development of this market in all aspects.

LED technology will help farmers increase yields. Positive radio wavelengths will shorten hospital stays. Brightness and color variations will help people relax or concentrate on demand. Store managers will be able to measure how lighting styles affect sales. Soon, LEDs will come fitted with sensors that "know" where and when to trigger such and such lighting effect. As Jon Gertner puts it, "The initial appeal of innovation doesn't predict the problems it may one day solve."[10]

## McDonald's: Local Citizen

Innovating in CSR can lead companies to innovate throughout. A new breeze in corporate responsibility will turn into a new breeze through the everyday life of a business. Take McDonald's France, for instance. Few divisions in the world have grown so steadily over the last fifteen years.

This despite the fact that, in 1999, the company had to face two major upsets that could have unsettled it for a long time. In the spring of that year, José Bové, a well-known French anti-global activist, directed an attack against one of its restaurants located in the small, southern French town of Millau. This attack was designed to publicize the supposedly evil consequences the restaurant's opening would have on local food and farming. Then, in the fall of the same year, mad cow disease sent a tremor through the beef market as people became fearful that beef and consequently hamburgers might be contaminated.

Against all odds, these two events acted as a wake-up call to McDonald's, changing the company's behavior for the better. This was no time to cower in a corner. Fast food has long been seen as undesirable in a country proud of its gastronomic tradition. The right reaction was transparency: telling people what McDonald's was about and offering exemplary CSR policies.

McDonald's France engaged in a wide range of actions to demonstrate a commitment to civic responsibility. A charter was signed with the farming community. Attention was drawn to the company's innovative youth employment policies. Product traceability was guaranteed. Relationships were established with the Ministry of Education and within the academic world. A joint research program was set up with an association of French pediatricians to study children's nutrition issues. An aid program for young farmers was founded. Ecologically designed packaging was introduced.

Other initiatives were even more startling. Here are three among many. McDonald's used frying oil is now recycled into organic diesel oil. Seventeen trucks run by McDonald's logistics partner Martin Browser now use this fuel. Secondly, restaurant employees and their managers are now being offered a recognized diploma after several years' service with McDonald's, in partnership with the Ministry of Education. The scale runs up as high as a university degree (available to restaurant managers). Finally, contracts have been signed with a startling 980 towns and villages in France to improve garbage-collection in the public domain. In short, McDonald's has become an exemplary member of the communities it inhabits.

But the thing I most want to draw attention to here, is the cumulative effect of these policies within the company. It seems that almost every McDonald's employee has adopted this new culture of innovation as her or his own. Throughout the company hierarchy, a perceptible desire for innovation has grown, as has a shared interest in finding new ways to improve consumer experience and keep the brand contemporary.

Product developers have invented, to name but a few: whole-wheat bun Big Macs, three towering Signature by McDonald's burgers, a Charolais burger and a kiwi-fruit lollipop. Marketing executives have found ways to make fruits and vegetables more appetizing to kids. Half the vegetables French kids eat in restaurants are consumed at a McDonald's. They get to choose a book or a toy in their *Happy Meal* menu. A collection of clothes has been designed for teenagers, on sale only at Colette, Paris's glamorous rue Saint-Honoré concept store. Restaurant designers have introduced pre-ordering terminals and table service. McDonald's now uses only recycled paper and encourages its customers to sort waste. Exterior design has been overhauled to suit local architectural paradigms. The first McDonald's restaurant in France to have received its HQE (high environmental quality) certificate has just opened. All new McDonald's restaurants are LED-lit.

And now McDonald's France's is working on a project they are not even sure they can pull off: a 100 percent energy-self-sufficient prototype restaurant.

## Super U: Local Sourcing

Another brand in France means a lot to me: a brand that combines a concern for the common good and for the environment with a strong commitment to growth. This is Système U, a coalition of independent supermarket owners, in competition with chains like Carrefour and Auchan. Over the last ten years, its market share has been the fastest growing in the country.

Système U works in a unique way. Private-label food products, for instance, must come from a radius of less than sixty miles from the store. No other company, it seems, is better at optimizing purchasing policy in favor of local sourcing. Système U supports nearly one thousand French organic milk farms. It protects rural employment by selling quality produce with a strong local identity. It won't sell endangered-species fish. It scrimps on any sort of excess, starting with packaging. It backs sustainable farming as far as it can without undermining productivity. Finally, it has committed to ridding its products of any substances or residues, which, though authorized, may be thought to represent a health risk. This is a huge and decisive step. What the French call the "precautionary principle" is applied throughout every store.

Système U's motto, *U, le commerce qui profite à tous* roughly translates as: "U, everyone profits." This means the business takes every stakeholder's interest into account: suppliers, distributors and consumers. Achieving this involves continual innovation. U has had a whole series of firsts. For years and years, remember, retailers were content to, well, just sell. Innovation came from their suppliers, mostly large companies. Nowadays, in many areas, it is the retailers who are ahead of the game. They are the innovators.

To Toms, McDonald's and Système U, CSR is not just icing on the cake. It stands at the heart of what they do. More and more companies are following their lead. Classic profit-driven corporations do not hesitate to invest in innovative civic projects that will end up boosting profits. Private and public concerns are coming together. Business and social requirements are standing side by side.

The public purse is increasingly empty. Now that corporations are tying their interests to the common good; now that their ideas are making people's lives easier; they need to step into the breach. And they can well afford to do so.

**Hence the questions:**

What if you considered corporate social responsibility not as a philanthropic initiative, but as a way to reinforce your core business?

What if your business became a part of the local community—in every one of your countries?

# 9

# Revival-Based Disruption

In the seventies, during the quartz watch revolution, senior executives from Zenith ordered that the molds for their mechanical watches be ditched. They were obsolete. One person at Zenith thought "I'll keep them in memory of times gone by"— times when, day after day, he and his workmates manufactured unique timepieces with remarkable craft skills. Zenith's executives today should congratulate that person. Analog watches, and other "outdated" products like fountain pens, streetcars, Burberry trench coats, and new-look bookstores fighting back against Amazon have become part of a past that is experiencing a resurrection today.

Ryan L. Raffaelli, assistant professor at the Harvard Business School puts it this way: "The key to success lies in redefining the product's value and meaning,"[1] adding that Swiss watchmakers have succeeded in making their mechanical watches not just timekeepers, but emblematic status symbols. The fact that a mechanical watch is so much more complicated to make than a digital watch lends symbolic worth, way beyond financial value.

From San Diego to Paris, streetcars are making a comeback because they are a green solution to urban transport problems. And bookstores are, well, real places to meet and talk about books—and anything else. Old products come back, when they are adapted to suit the times. This is the spirit of vintage. It is called revival innovation. Even more interesting to me is the phenomenon of rediscovered technologies that may not have succeeded in their day but are given a second chance now to become "sudden" hits.

Workshops and labs are full of old ideas desperate to see the light of day. 3M's research department had a glue that didn't stick very well. . . . A few years later, a researcher came up with a new way of using it. He called the product "Post-it." I mentioned light-emitting diodes, LEDs, in the last chapter. They had been on Philips's low-priority agenda for fifty years, a kind of secondary priority. Until one day, when someone was told to make the project work within twelve months, or scrap it.

## Apple: No-Future Front Glass

Everyone has experienced that sudden, unexpected, decisive moment. Like Steve Jobs when he visited Corning Glass. The glass face for the iPhone and iPad, an absolute revolution in screen technology, was actually discovered a full half-century earlier at Corning. They had let their invention idle away in a drawer, certain it had no future.

Corning engineer Donald Stookey had discovered or invented Pyroceram by mistake. This was the first ceramic glassware ultra-resistant against knocks and scratches. Ten years later, Corning used Stookey's findings to inspire a research project that came up with glass that was fifteen times stronger than any other. But nobody wanted it. Production ceased in 1991. The technology involved was forgotten.

Apple, meanwhile, was seeking a glass manufacturer able to produce absolutely scratchproof glass to equip what was to become the iPhone. Steve Jobs's teams met every single glass-manufacturing company they could find, big and small, to no avail. No glass, no iPhone.

When the people from Cupertino showed up at Corning, some engineers dug out of a dusty drawer what was to become "Gorilla Glass." Today, this uniquely resistant glass, less than a mere millimeter thick, is what covers the front of the iPhone and the iPad. The glass Steve Jobs made Corning bring back to life is now standard on some nine hundred different models belonging to thirty-three different brands. It contributes more than a billion dollars to Corning's turnover.

## Roosegaarde: Smart Highways

Slow down the shutter speed as you snap cars driving along a highway at night. What you get is long red and yellow stripes. Rear lights, front lights.

Now imagine you are driving down that same highway at night. Reflective lines on either side are there to guide you, like the ones in the photo. They are called "Glowing Lines," part of a "Smart Highway" project that will make highway lighting redundant.

Innovation in the motor transport sector is usually thought to relate to cars. Rarely to infrastructure. But one Dutch designer and his engineer partner have turned their attention to road systems. Their idea is to link four innovative road schemes. First: phosphorescent road markings known as "Glow-in-the-Dark Lining," a substitute for highway streetlights making for a huge reduction in power consumption. Second: smartpaint on road surfaces, to indicate, for instance, weather conditions. A snowflake might warn against black ice, for example. Accidents and bottleneck warnings would come up too. Third: "Wind Light" turbines to harness vehicle wind power as cars speed by and thus light roadsides interactively, meaning self-sufficiently. The road network would illuminate itself. Four: one lane would be a priority lane for electric cars. It would recharge their batteries as they drive along. If this project by the Roosegaarde design team ever comes to fruition, the outcome will be fascinating.

"Smart Highway" relates to revival innovation in two ways. The technology allowing road surfaces to become luminous is thirty years old. The idea is to incorporate solar power crystals into paint. Aside from use in a baby bath mat that changes color according to water temperature, this technology has never really found an added-value application. The same is true for magnetic fields placed beneath a road surface to recharge electric cars.

"Smart Highway" is an avant-garde idea that will make roads safer, more environmentally friendly and more beautiful. For the most part, the technology is old. And the timing is perfect. "Smart Highway" has emerged just as connected cars with their onboard navigation systems are going to hook up to intelligent roads. And at a time when many governments have decided to save energy by switching streetlights off late at night along highways, in public spaces and even city streets.

## NeoLucida: Revisiting the Nineteenth Century

In the middle of the nineteenth century, artists like Ingres were still using the camera lucida, a remarkable optical tool that was basically a prism on a sliding mount. Artists could look through the prism and see their subject projected onto a flat surface and thus sketch out what they wanted to paint. In other words, even old masters relied on technical support, a form of assistance eventually replaced by photography.

Well, maybe not. As the authors of *Big Bang Disruption*[2] wrote, Pablo Garcia and Golan Levin, art professors, have recently pioneered a new version of the camera lucida called NeoLucida. The interesting thing is that this device has been developed not by an optical company but by two art professors.

The authors also pointed out[3] that what the professors have done is go back into the past and resurrect an old product by applying innovative contemporary design. First, their product was conceived using open-source software. All the components they needed were found on the Internet. Optics and distribution were outsourced. Not just that. The financing needed, some $400,000, was raised on the funding platform Kickstarter.[4] Finally, they never intended to make money. Their aim was to offer artists an invaluable aid. All the information you need to build a NeoLucida is available to everyone via a Creative Commons–type open-source platform.

In other words, a device that became obsolete in the nineteenth century has found a new lease of life in the open economy. It has gained "A Second Wind," to quote the title of a piece in *The Economist* about re-emergent technologies.

**Hence the questions:**

What if you re-looked at all your abandoned projects in the context of today?

What if a product from the past could acquire a different, symbolic value in today's world?

What if you made proprietary technology available to all on Creative Commons?

## CHAPTER

# 10

# Data-Driven Disruption

Take a candy jar. One of those giant clear glass candy jars with a big, flat, round stopper you see in old-fashioned candy stores. It has got hundreds, maybe thousands of pieces of candy in it. Someone asks, "So how many pieces of candy does the jar contain?" The chances are you won't get the right answer. You will be wrong by a wide margin. But if lots of people are asked the same question and an average of their answers is taken, the figure reached will prove astonishingly close. At first sight this seems more than improbable. Statisticians, though, are familiar with the principle. It is called "The Wisdom of Crowds."

In 2013, one of our agencies in Australia applied this to predicting the outcome of the Melbourne Cup, a race that brings together the best thoroughbreds in the world. We collated all the tweets we could find about all the horses in the race, as well as their trainers and jockeys. We recorded all the favorable comments we could find, tens of thousands of them, about each of the entries. This process produced what you might call an Internet favorite, a horse called "Fiorente." The bookies' odds on Fiorente were not all that hot. The horse was far from favorite.

It won the race.

Statistical evidence of this sort shows that we all share in some kind of collective, subterranean intelligence. Data, you could say, teaches us how to apprehend reality. Utilizing data increases our chances of success in any undertaking. And this fact opens up opportunities for innovation.

The *New York Times* home page, for instance, offers readers instant access to the pieces most likely to interest them: both bespoke news coverage and favorite columnists. Readers are also sent iPhone or iPad alerts. This way, a powerful newspaper constantly refuels its data bank. Indeed, no other newspaper in the world boasts so many Facebook and Twitter friends and followers. It even uses a data-analysis tool to single out influential tweets and help let editors know when the time is right to upload a piece.

## The Weather Company: The World's Most Data-Rich System

Data is driving the profound transformation business is undergoing. Take *The Weather Channel*. Thirty years ago, *The Weather Channel* was just a television forecasting service. Today, *The Weather Company* provides airline, insurance, and pharmaceutical companies, not to mention retail and wholesale distributors, with applications derived from its weather-predictive know-how. *Contagious* magazine[1] tells us that *The Weather Company* knows when a dew-percentage threshold will trigger Texas insecticide sales and will teach you that more yogurt gets eaten on bright winter days. As Vikram Somaya, *The Weather Channel* managing director, puts it: "We tap into the world's most data-rich complex system, the weather."[2]

These days of course, data has accumulated to such dizzying heights that it is termed "big data." The term is used with abandon, but it does reflect the new reality. We do have much more data now than we could ever imagine. We also use them much faster, and much more cheaply, than in the past, in spite of the fact that they have become increasingly complex. Our new standard measure of digital information is the exabyte. This is a one followed by eighteen zeros. It describes the entire range of data gathered over just one year. Eric E. Schmidt, Google's executive chairman, has this to say about it: "Every two days now we create as much information as we did from the dawn of civilization up until 2003."[3] We are definitely going to need unlimited capacity systems to store all that.

Big-data collection has a corollary that affects us all. Everything we do is permanently under surveillance. University-trained brains, usually masters of data science, a new discipline in many of the world's best places of learning, oversee hundreds of millions of dollars' worth of expenditure designed to generate new and better ways of exploiting the huge potential that data constitutes. Every day, these data scientists invent new and innovative algorithms. The return on this investment is considerable. In 2013, a Bain report[4] underlined the competitive edge gained by corporations that have invested massively in big data. According to this study, such corporations are twice as likely to be in the most profitable quartile of world companies.[5] Above all, the insights—meaning the intuitive understanding of customer wishes—that data offers, help these corporations make their decisions much faster. Five times faster in fact.

## Amazon: Related-Purchases System

Not many companies are in Amazon's league when it comes to using knowledge of customers to generate highly personalized recommendations. Amazon's "related purchases" system has been copied the world over—by Netflix and Uber, not least.

Under this system, a virtuous circle is created. Quality products and services attract buyers, who provide data that goes into improving products and services. No one understands customer purchase patterns like Amazon. Few other companies dare go as far as the e-commerce platform: it has even patented an anticipatory package shipping system. Its ability to use predictive assessment to evaluate customer practice is so precise that it can start preparing delivery before a purchase is even made!

One Sunday night, not many months ago, I had an Uber taxi meet me at the station on my way home from Avignon. I found the service impeccable. Competitively priced. Until that day, I had thought of Uber as just another highly effective taxi service. Naively, I had no idea it would soon be competing, in its own way, with Facebook, Google, Apple or Microsoft.

The reality is that if, one day, you need to leave home early to get to the office, then have an urgent client meeting across town, then see a close friend for lunch, then head back to the office, before hooking up with your wife at the theater in the evening, Uber will know. As Ron Hirson puts it in his *Forbes* magazine blog, "There are only four people/organizations in the world who know my location at all times: my wife (because I tell her); Apple (because of Siri); the NSA (because it's the NSA); and now Uber. Uber, he adds, knows where you live, where you work, where you go on vacation, the restaurants you like and the gyms you choose."[6]

As far as Uber is concerned, we, its customers, are not just passengers. We have not been just passengers for a long time. We are the company's principal asset. We fuel its incomparable database, which may soon be up there with Facebook's and Microsoft's databases, and become an inexhaustible source of secondary revenue from hotels and airlines. Big data has opened up a whole new world for Uber. Employees, customers and shareholders can look forward to a very bright future. Uber was established in 2009, and its estimated worth is currently $50 billion.[7]

## KBC: The Gap in the Market

Data scientists are everywhere these days: in every business and every corporation, regardless of size or nationality. Even in ad agencies. At TBWA we have developed a truly innovative program for a Belgian client, KBC bank. We call this program "The Gap in the Market."

Starting your own business is never easy. Having the boldness is not always enough, nor even is having a great idea. Sometimes, you also need to find the right location. Which is why we suggested to KBC that a tool could help detect local businesses in search of funding. We came up with something called "The Gap Finder Tool." This "smart" community platform crowdsources local business opportunities, aggregates the data and makes it rapidly available to local business starters.

Just fill out your zip code and indicate what businesses are absent from your neighborhood. This will tell potential entrepreneurs where they might want to set up and what locations might be suitable to their needs. All they have to do then is publish details of their proposed business on the website. Throughout Flanders, local residents have shown themselves to be very prompt in reacting to proposals.

Initially, we exposed "The Gap Finder Tool" through TV and radio advertising. Every town had its own, constantly updated ad. Vacant store-windows in the best shopping areas were covered in posters telling passersby to check out the website. A partnership with local correspondents from a national newspaper guaranteed a stream of articles that outlined the specific needs of each city, no matter what size.

So what was the result? Suddenly every newspaper, TV, and radio station in the country took up the story of how there was a shortage of neighborhood stores. No less than 171,157 gaps in the market were identified, an average of 560 per village or town. Nearly 1,500 new business ideas emerged, in a region of no more than seven million inhabitants! The website was initially intended as a campaign tool, but soon it became a valuable data bank for anyone planning on starting a business, and an exchange forum in its own right. The data we have gathered has proved extremely useful, both to KBC and cities with needs.

Now our scheme is reaching a new stage. We are cross-referencing the information we have gathered with facts gleaned in other preexisting data banks to refine our gap analysis even further. The idea is that, every morning of his or her working life, every bank manager in the land should be provided with the address of two people wanting to start up a business and the best location for that business. The two prospects will be clearly identified and perfectly qualified.

Two people a day? The beauty of this initiative is the incredible precision it will achieve, making data really smart.

Where Internet was good for small companies, however, smart data will privilege larger ones. The Internet was good for starts-ups and small businesses because it opened a new world of opportunities to them. But nowadays, smart data is offering big corporations a living pool of facts and information, which smaller and younger firms cannot access. And this advantage is becoming overwhelmingly significant. As Amazon and Microsoft, but also Procter & Gamble and General Electric tell us, tomorrow's innovation will be more and more data-driven.

And in case anyone is not convinced—in case anyone has not seen just how big smart data is—I will close with a quote from a McKinsey "big data" report. "If U.S. healthcare were to use big data creatively and effectively to drive efficiency and quality, the sector could create more than $300 billion in value every year."[8]

That says it all.

**Hence the questions:**

What if you endlessly strived to transform your data into smart data?

What if on top of your core activity, you became a data supplier?

What if you built your customer relations on a related-purchases scheme like Amazon?

# 11

# Usage-Based Disruption

When I became account executive on the Ariel account, I was asked to write a note on the brand's latest "Usage and Attitude" survey. Back then, Procter & Gamble ran two such studies a year with a market research company, that sent inspectors into hundreds of homes to monitor how consumers lived with their products. We would sit feverishly waiting for the results, in the knowledge that we would be expected to interpret them and come up with recommendations.

Several decades later, old-style "Usage and Attitude" reports have given way to studies that try to get much closer to consumers. Closer to what Procter & Gamble calls "The second moment of truth," i.e., when consumers use the product, the first moment of truth being the act of purchasing. Procter & Gamble products are consumed three billion times every day so, not surprisingly, observing customers closely is P&G's main source of inspiration.

## Haier: From Anomaly to Innovation

Zhang Ruimin is the highly charismatic chairman of Haier, the world's largest supplier of white goods (meaning washing machines and fridges). *Fortune* magazine has claimed that Zhang is "innovating radically, maybe more radically than any other manager operating on such a large scale."[1] How? By making Haier totally alert to any observation that might be of use to them, especially when it is unexpected or even disturbing.

Here is a much-reported story that features in many books on innovation. A rural customer complains his washing machine is broken. Haier sends someone to investigate, who discovers that the customer is using the machine to clean his freshly dug potatoes. Haier headquarters is informed. The engineers there understand they have stumbled on an opportunity to satisfy a whole range of customers, since the complainant cannot be the only one to have thought of rinsing vegetables in a washing machine. Soon after, the world's first ever machine that cleans both clothes and vegetables is put on the market. Initially, the device's awkwardly big tubes were a laughingstock, especially outside China. But Haier sold more than half a million of them.

Uncovering information fast, however odd that information might seem, is the hallmark of Haier. Its eighty thousand staff members are encouraged to keep in close and constant touch with customers. They work in small, horizontal crews that function as independent, grassroots profit centers. The firm currently boasts more than four thousand such non-hierarchical units.

Any recommendation put forward by any member of staff is subject to a vote, not only inside the company, but also with customers and suppliers. If the idea is approved—and here is what many observers describe as Haier's avant-garde management method—its initiator is then put in charge of making it happen. He or she chooses a team. A hierarchy is established. But only as long as it takes to complete the project. Ruimin says: "It is important to keep twirling the pyramid all the time, because it is important employees listen to the market and not to the boss."[2]

Haier owns ten thousand registered patents.[3] Its turnover is constantly growing. The lengthy list of its innovations is staggering. For example: a freezer that can go one hundred hours without power (very useful for Africa), a washbasin with facial recognition (to ensure the hot water is just as you like it) and headphones equipped with a remote control system that lets you program your TV set by brainpower alone. As for the potato-washing machine, surprisingly it spawned a powder-free clothes washing machine, launched in 2009.[4] This truly disruptive technology has rapidly propelled Haier to become the top supplier to laundries in China and around the world.

Chairman Ruimin has created China's first global brand. Chinese bloggers regard him as a hero. The *Forbes* magazine piece on him carried the following headline. "Wisdom from the Oracle of Qingdao."[5] Not bad for a former Red Guard.

## M-Pesa: A Bank in Your Phone

Let us now move from China and its rising middle class to Africa's underprivileged populations. Close observation of usage has inspired disruptive innovation in Africa too. Or rather, close observation of non-usage, caused by lack of infrastructure.

Finding a bank branch in this immense continent often involves traveling for miles. Nine out of ten Africans, in any case, lack the resources to join a bank. A large majority, on the other hand, own a mobile phone.

This is what prompted Vodafone to launch M-Pesa, an innovative money-transfer service that uses mobile phones. It allows millions of people without a bank account to send and receive money, to buy phone credit, pay bills and even find loans. "I don't need to go to the bank when I have the bank in my phone" says one customer. All you need to do is register with your service provider. Then walk into any Vodafone shop, pharmacy or gas station, to turn your cash into electronic money. Anyone receiving money can reverse the operation at will.

M-pesa represents the vanguard of smartphones becoming pay terminals. As in India and China, most of Africa's young people will never use a landline. Many won't ever know a credit card. More than 70 percent of adults in Kenya have signed up for M-pesa.[6] That is ten times more than those who have a bank account.

Such a remarkable degree of penetration is not just a great sales success, it compensates for lack of infrastructure. M-pesa makes transactions more fluid. It facilitates exchange. Many businesses would not exist without it.

## Wibbitz: Texts into Videos

An idea can come from just looking at how people use their mobile phones, their tablets, and other connected tools. That is what the founders of Wibbitz did, who want to revolutionize the way we get our news. They take advantage of the increasingly widespread use of mobile devices to access news and of users' growing interest in interactive video. They know which are the most watched and shared.

Wibbitz is the bold start-up behind the app of the same name. *BBC News*, *The Guardian*, *The Telegraph*, *The Huffington Post*, and *Forbes* are among the hundred press organizations and news websites that have agreed to work with it. Wibbitz is a magical device that makes a video out of a text. It transforms written pieces into television news. The algorithm it contains "reads" pieces in the dailies and magazines and turns them into one- or two-minute films. The images are mined out of unlimited-access video-image banks. Synthesized voiceover speaks key sentences from the written text. The quality of these automatically generated films is almost perfect. Just take a look at videos on Jay Z, Jennifer Lawrence, or Angela Merkel.

Start-ups do not get much attention in these pages because my main focus is on how big corporations are lacking in innovation. I mention Wibbitz because it is emblematic of a certain type of company, and they are many, whose success is based on a simple observation of how we use digital technology.

## Burberry: Walking into a Website

Some companies, though, go further. To them, online dictates offline. Burberry has seen sales triple since it adopted this approach. From dusty and antiquated, the brand has reconquered an eminent place in the world of luxury. Not only that: sleek new Burberry has also catapulted London back into one of the fashion capitals of the world, after years in the doldrums.

In a *Harvard Business Review* interview, Angela Ahrendts, the CEO who oversaw this spectacular comeback, puts it simply. "This is how customers live. They wake up with a device in their hand and life begins."[7] So she broke down the barriers between our real and our digital existences, a decision that has spawned innovative idea upon innovative idea.

At Burberry you can design your own bespoke coat, based on hundreds of different available options. You can choose buttons, stitch, thickness of lining and match different fabrics. In the store, many items carry a label. Press that label and a video starts, showing how Burberry staff craft the clothes they make.

Burberry joined Facebook in 2009. The brand's twenty million fans[8] now exchange news about events and store openings, about fashion shows and backstage gossip. Those shows are streamed live. Two million Internet users watch them.[9] They can also purchase items at a click. The clothes are delivered a few weeks later. Burberry calls this service "runway to reality."[10]

These ideas and many others were exemplified when the brand's flagship Regent Street store opened in London. The decor reflects the design of the website; real life as home page. The ground floor is divided into "Bespoke," "Acoustic" and "Experiences," just like the home page. "Walking through the doors," says Angela Ahrendts, "is just like walking into our Web site."[11] When you walk through that store, it feels like clicking on the real world.

Everything the company does in its stores and its workshops or at its shows, is dictated by its online existence. Burberry has turned the logic upside down.

**Hence the questions:**

What if your online activities dictated your offline offering?

What if you let unexpected usage of your products inspire new product design?

What if you understood better how people relate to your products through their connected devices?

# CHAPTER

# 12

# Price-Led Disruption

At *Berliner Republik*, a beer hall in the German capital, the price of a glass of beer varies according to the time of day, depending on demand. Customers can see prices rising or falling on screens. The fewer people there are, the lower the price.

It used to be that products were sold for a fixed price outside specific and limited sales times. Today, price fluctuations seem normal, because hotels, airlines, railway companies, and car rental firms all engage in yield management. These companies use the previous year's reservations to establish price models. They can predict the seasonality of demand rising and falling and model their prices accordingly—even, on occasion, down to giving the product away for free.

This book is about disruptive approaches to marketing, so I hardly have anything to say about disruptive technology or innovation based on technical breakthroughs here. Nonetheless, it is true that lower prices, which are happening across a broad range of sectors, are the consequence of what are known as exponential technologies. These are technologies that improve rapidly, with costs decreasing in parallel even more rapidly. Capacity doubles every eighteen months according to Moore's Law. Hence the exponential pace of progress and sophistication, whether in computing, in genetics, in biotechnology or nano-technology. In each of these fields exponential technologies are helping generate a broad range of disruptive innovations.

Yet new technologies are far from being the only source of price competitiveness. An approach that is especially effective for those wanting to reduce their cost of sales is to re-evaluate their offer by breaking it down. This opens up an alternative. Either they pare down the product or service by removing nonessential elements, such as with the low-cost car or airline business models, or they offer one part for free. This is what music and video streaming platforms do.

## Logan: Art of Unbundling

What sparked everything off was a visit made by Louis Schweit-zer, then head of the French car manufacturer Renault, to Russia in the late nineties. He noticed that ten years after the fall of the Berlin Wall, ancient Soviet Lada cars were still very popular. This made him realize that there was a market for cheap cars, but he deplored that in those days technical innovations could not be included in a six-thousand-euro package. "I wrote a list of essential specifications," he told the authors of *Jugaad*,[1] "that can be summarized in three words: modern, reliable, affordable. The rest, I added, was negotiable."

Western engineers tend to seek sophistication for its own sake. They think making things more complex is progress. But the average purchaser uses only a limited part of a car's functions. Renault designed the Logan by going against the grain of classic research and engineering methods. The car has become its lead product and not just in emerging markets.

Ryanair got rid of various services offered by most airlines: airport proximity, baggage registration, in-flight drinks and meals. This "unbundling" has made Ryanair tickets very cheap. Profits come from separately billed services. If you use all of these separately billed services, you end up with less of a bargain, even though the initial ticket price may have been very low. All the same, Irish-based Ryanair has been a big success. No other airline in Europe carries more passengers.

"Unbundling," then redesigning an offer is obviously easier in the service sector than in manufacturing. It is harder to achieve for Renault than for Ryanair. However, the service sector has its own challenges. Because competitors can adjust their business model in a moment, each company needs to control everything down to the tiniest detail to always stay ahead of the field.

## Spotify: The Freemium Model

Another way of innovating in terms of price is the so-called Freemium model.

Spotify, a Swedish company that possesses the world's biggest music catalogue offers free, limited access in the hope of turning new listeners into subscribers. Free listening time is limited to ten hours per month. No piece can be heard more than five times. You might think such constraints would put customers off. They do, but the offer is so attractive that users enjoy the platform, and cannot bring themselves to forego subscribing. It is a delicate balance. This kind of business model generates the subscription levels it needs by understanding people's frustration. As a result, Spotify has gone from 7 million users in Europe in 2010, including 250,000 paid subscribers, to 75 million users worldwide in 2015, of which 20 million had subscribed. That year, Spotify contributed $3 billion to the music business in royalties.[2]

## ZipDial: Making Money Out of Free Products and Services

Indians are addicted to "number withheld" services. They have diverted mobile phones from their intended use by letting a number ring two or three times before hanging up. Ending the call before anyone picks up allows free communication. All sorts of messages can be transmitted in this way, such as letting someone know you are going to be late for a meeting, that you are back home safely or merely that you are thinking about the person you have called.

ZipDial has seized upon this unintended usage to establish a startling business model that monetizes such calls. The idea is that Indian consumers can beep into a brand by dialing a dedicated "withheld call" line. ZipDial returns the call or sends out a text message outlining recent promotional offers.

This service has won over more than three hundred companies including Unilever, Disney, and L'Oréal. Gillette has more than three million ZipDial users, yet "only" two million "likes" on Facebook.[3] And Twitter has allowed people without smartphones to get celebrity tweets by dialing a ZipDial number. Evidence, if ever there was, that social networks can live without the Internet.

The concept of price has evolved considerably. In the old days, it related to quality. It defined the value of the product on offer for the duration. Today, a lot more is expected of price. The price of a product is part and parcel of its evolving commercial career. Price variations provide a broad palette of conversion-based pricing options and customer loyalty programs. This has overturned many assumptions that seemed set in stone.

Until now, the fundamental basis for any transaction—price—was set by the seller. Today, Priceline and other similar platforms have launched a "Name-Your-Own-Price" trend. Just a few years ago, who would have imagined agreeing to pay for a hotel without knowing its name? Or a flight without knowing its route, even at a very competitive price? Priceline lets you have the information only once you have paid.

In the past, price was hardly inspiring. Sure, it needed to be selected with care, because it established the value of something that was new. Today, because price can vary in real time and modulate according to a range of criteria, it is no longer just a dry, cold number. It is a key element of disruptive business models—and a source of creativity.

**Hence the questions:**

What if you decided to offer part of your products and services for free?

What if you "unbundled" the products you sell and only kept what is essential?

What if you added a time limit to your product offering?

# 13

# Added-Service Disruption

In this Internet age, products are becoming services and services are becoming products. More exactly: material goods are increasingly augmented with related services. And services are often embodied within a physical object.

Some six or seven years ago, an app called Hello Baby[1] attracted my notice. It offered a two-minute video showing how the fetus grows every week. The images were riveting. In week eighteen, a tiny human being acquires fingers. Ten weeks later, he can be seen reacting to exterior sounds. This video was produced by Pampers just a few months after the first smartphone apps emerged. Mothers could download the app and add personal details, including baby due date, gender, size, and weight and so chart week-by-week development. And share their baby's progress with their friends on Facebook.

An African proverb states, "It takes a village to raise a child."[2] So Pampers has built a "Pampers Village" for the digital era on its website. Mothers sign up to find all kinds of useful advice about pregnancy and the first months of a newborn's life, including nutrition, safety, sleep, and skincare . . .

Basically, Procter & Gamble has chosen to add services to its products in order to make them more useful. The company expects every one of its brands to offer not just a functional benefit—in the case of Pampers, drier bottoms—but also to acquire a purpose. In other words, the Pampers brand, beyond product benefits, does what it can to help smooth babies' growth and improve mothers' welfare.

Programs and apps like Hello Baby are rooted in the "brand-utility" concept. Nike has brilliantly illustrated this trend over nearly ten years with its "Nike+ Fuelband," a service so appreciated by its thirty million users that CEO Mark Parker now describes his brand's universe as "digital sport."[3] The way it works forms a circle, from sneakers to associated service, itself embodied in a physical bracelet.

"Fast followers"—companies that are the first to imitate innovative enterprises—are so quick off the mark that it is hard for the trailblazers to keep ahead of the game. Commoditization is the underlying danger. One way of avoiding or at least delaying this threat, inherent in technological proliferation, is by coming up with a service. Added services initiate conversations between brand and customer. They build customer loyalty.

Jean-Paul Agon, the Chairman and CEO of L'Oréal, thinks that usefulness is part of beauty. "The digital revolution is changing the nature of what we offer," he once declared in a press interview. "Until now, we sold only products. From now on, we will be selling a combination of product together with a related service."[4] Tutorials help customers improve their mascara- and foundation-application skills. They teach women how wrinkles come about and strengthen their ability to fight the effects of stress, pollution or menopause on skin. This skincare advice is rooted in the "Science of Beauty," a concept that lies at the very heart of what L'Oréal stands for.

So "added service" is a fertile concept. McCormick, the spice company has launched "FlavorPrint," a service whose algorithm matches customer taste with a range of flavors to generate bespoke shopping lists. *Harvard Business Review* said, "'Flavor-Print' does for recipes what Netflix has done for movies."[5] KLM Airline has a "Meet & Seat" app that lets you hook up with compatible fellow-passengers, people who share your interests or are traveling to the same event as you: a concert, an exhibition or a conference. Share your Facebook or LinkedIn profile and find out where those people are sitting.

In retailing, service quality is what differentiates between companies. Carrefour makes shopping easier with a sat-nav app that locates products on its shelves. Hubert Joly runs Best Buy, the company that created Twelpforce and that now owns the Geek Squad. He says, "We believe that price-competitiveness is table stakes. The way we want to win is around the advice, convenience, service."[6] Best Buy proves its commitment to having the best service on offer, by giving Internet advice to people who are not even customers. Not yet anyway.

Three years ago, our Finnish agency developed "Window Shopping" for Adidas. Our creative technologists developed interactive store windows. We even trademarked the prototype. Consumers can play with these windows, turning them into product display screens, from which to select and reserve goods as they might with an iPad.

In this instance, as with most of the examples I have given, digital opens up a thousand opportunities when it comes to enriching an original offer by adding services. The most exciting developments in technology will not just be defined in terms of what we can achieve virtually but what we can do to enhance the physical world by overlaying seamless digital experiences.

## Darty: 3.0 Customer Service

What do a magnet on your refrigerator that lets you order pizzas, a connected button that watches over your white goods and instantly calls customer service when something goes wrong, and a "smart" pillbox that helps your doctor oversee your medication from afar, all have in common? Each one embodies excellence of service within a physical object.

In 2012, we recommended that Red Tomato Pizza launch a VIP Fridge Magnet in Dubai. This is a gadget that connects with the nearest Red Tomato Pizza branch. At the touch of a button, your favorite pizza is ordered and delivered within minutes.

In the summer of 2014, Darty, the largest French white-goods retailing company, announced a breakthrough in customer service when it launched its "Red Button," a device connected to any domestic appliance. If an appliance runs into a problem, all you need to do is press that button. A Darty representative will connect by phone almost immediately. No more hours spent running through what the problem might be: all the necessary information is available to that representative online. Darty Customer Service can send a repairman very rapidly. Better still, Darty's "Red Button" will report on the condition of your appliances in real time and thus warn of any prospective problems. The Red Button completely fulfills the promise in Darty's vintage slogan, "*Le Contrat de Confiance*,"[7] a phrase that translates as "the Trust Contract." And in this way, Darty's after-sales service offering has entered the 3.0 era.

As Chris Anderson says in *Makers*, as soon as someone comes up with a service idea, it only takes a few lines of code to turn it into reality.[8] And to deliver it to millions of individuals around the world, at the touch of a button.

## Medissimo: Smart Pillboxes

Connected objects are becoming increasingly familiar in the health care field, as a means of extending medical supervision beyond hospitals and clinics.

Forgetting to take your medication costs society money. The New England Healthcare Institute thinks $290 billion is wasted every year in the United States alone by people not taking their drugs. That represents 13 percent of all public health care expenditure.[9] In France, more than a million hospital days a year could be saved by people taking their medicine as prescribed. Smart pillboxes may help solve that problem.

Medissimo has partnered with Bouygues Telecom to launch a pillbox that monitors people's medication intake at a distance. An alarm reminds patients it is time to take their next pill. The patient's entourage, mainly doctors and pharmacists, can check that a prescription is being followed as it should. And when someone takes the wrong pill, or forgets to take a pill, their pillbox is preprogrammed to send out an automated warning.

The Internet of Things is bringing back objects. A connected object is the visible part of an iceberg, which also includes the multitude of services embodied in that object. Connected pillboxes have been very well received. In 2014, they won the Innovation Trophy in the health care category at the CES Innovation Awards in Las Vegas.

## Allianz: The Penalty of Leadership

What is true of corporations that sell products is also true of service corporations. Standard offers need enriching.

Take insurance-company products and services. On the surface, they may seem uninspiring. Allianz, Europe's number one insurer, has decided to change that. Top-ranking companies have to behave as pioneers. This used to be called the "Penalty of Leadership"—the cost of staying at the top. A leader cannot afford to let rivals, sometimes even start-ups, take the initiative, as so many do. Which is why Allianz has devised a whole raft of innovative services.

In July 2014, for instance, Allianz launched an online connected automobile assistance service. A box that fits into your car, which, coupled with a smartphone app, offers true on-board intelligence. In case of an accident, it will dial up assistance automatically. It will also oversee your driving, letting you download information about how you drive: fuel consumption, braking and accelerating habits. The data goes into the box. Soon it will allow Allianz to establish a "Pay-How-You-Drive" service, a form of customized pricing that will lower premiums for good drivers and so free them from having to pay for bad ones.

Allianz has also found a whole range of new ways of renovating home insurance. The first is designed to facilitate settling theft and damages claims by mutual agreement. This is how it works: In November 2013, Allianz entered into an agreement with Amazon to set up a price reference system for groups of products. Once a claim is established, claimants are offered a choice of financial compensation or to resupply via Amazon. If the latter option is preferred, the claimant will then be offered a very wide range of new or used replacement products. In this case, Allianz's Amazon partnership will speed up claims processing impressively.

Allianz has also established a partnership with Nest, the "intelligent" home specialist, to offer home insurance coupled with smoke and carbon monoxide detection. This is called "Nest Protect." The alarm uses customers' mobile phones to warn them of the nature of a threat and tell them how dangerous it may be.

In other words, Allianz has introduced real, disruptive innovations across all areas of their activity. Inevitably, competitors will copy one or other of them. But by introducing them all simultaneously, it has given the market leader an impressive head start. Prospective clients are shown that, as far as Allianz is concerned, insurance companies are no longer doomed to live with their current poor image.

Allianz, L'Oréal, Procter & Gamble . . . Digital-driven improvements affect every corporation. They are stimulating sales. Making brands more relevant. Revolutionizing medicine and health care. Encouraging the insurance business to rethink how it works. And as we have seen with Darty and Best Buy, revitalizing the retail sector.

Seven years ago, Tesco's Home Plus subsidiary conducted the following experiment in Seoul. Life-size subway-station posters reproduced store shelves. Passengers could connect up a smartphone, order shopping online from the subway and have it delivered within hours. When customers use a mobile phone to scan a product's barcode on a poster in this way, they do not feel they are entering into a digital world. They feel the real world is digitizing.

A large number of new business models are based on this new seamlessness between the analog world and the digital world. Between tangible and intangible. Between online and offline. Between communication and what is being communicated.

Between products and services.

**Hence the questions:**

What if you added services to the physical products you sell?
And inversely:
What if you embodied the services you offer in a physical product?

# 14

# Partnership-Led Disruption

W e were sitting beside the Bosphorus, Levent Cakiroglu and I. Levent is chief executive of a big Turkish corporation named Beko, the number one firm in the European domestic-appliance sector and client of our Istanbul agency.

He told me he was about to hire a director of innovation. "Disruptive innovation," he pointed out, because however interesting his engineers' suggestions were, they were always incremental, never disruptive.

He was curious to know what I meant by Disruption. He asked me how we did things and how Disruption, as a concept, had evolved over time. I gave him detailed examples of the innovation exercises we organize during our "Disruption Days," with a particular emphasis on virtual partnerships. We use these sessions to devise unlikely partnerships that often turn out to be inspirational. Here's one example I gave. "Suppose you started a joint venture with L'Oréal. What product might you come up with together?"

The question was rhetorical, merely intended to illustrate how we function. All the same, he thought it over, stared into my eyes for a moment and exclaimed, "In hot countries, beauty products melt. I've noticed women often keep them in a refrigerator. I propose we devise a miniature, bedroom refrigerator for L'Oréal. Really elegant, like a pretty cigar box."

I was thrilled that the exercise had proved fertile and in just a few seconds. But I replied that his miniature refrigerator was just one little idea. The point of what we do is to come up with more impressive projects. Immediately, he answered my criticism with this: "You have no idea just how big this 'little idea' could be. Our company has been fighting its way out of the kitchen for half a century. This "little idea" would just let us into people's bedrooms."

Coming up with imaginary alliances often proves productive: an unexpected juxtaposition brings new ideas.

And what works theoretically is just as effective in real life.


## Sixt and BMW

BMW teamed up with car rental firm Sixt in 2011 to create an innovative car-sharing joint venture called DriveNow. Initially tested in Munich and Berlin, it has expanded to six other cities including London and San Francisco. BMW targets one million customers by 2020.

Needless to say, car sharing is an unexpected initiative from a car manufacturer. It could be seen as the wrong way to go. But this is how BMW is responding to the rise of the collaborative economy in which usage matters more than ownership.

In fact, this is an ingenious way of reaching two different generations simultaneously. A younger, more urban generation that has become less obsessed with the idea of buying its first car. And an older generation that can try out its BMWs in a new context, especially electric models, which are harder for them to get used to.

## Unexpected Alliances

BMW and Sixt operate in related sectors. McDonald's and Angry Birds don't. Nor do Uber and American Express or Lego and Warner Bros.

Unexpected partnerships between corporations like these, working in very different fields, also offer a favorable environment for innovation. Our Helsinki and Shanghai agencies (the former working closely with the people behind Angry Birds) came up with a remarkable initiative, a unique gaming experience, for McDonald's in China. The "Angry Burgers" promotion was so successful over the two months of its existence that the partnership between the firms came to appear as a natural match.

Establishing partnerships is the engine that drives American Express's business too. *Contagious* magazine[1] reports that Amex has signed dozens of partnership agreements. Such as with TripAdvisor, giving Amex cardholders, who are also TripAdvisor members, discounts, and promotional offers. Or Uber, letting passengers pay their fares with Amex cardholder rewards. Or Twitter—Amex Sync on Twitter has generated many ancillary partnerships. When they tweet, clients who sync their cards to Twitter can save on products and services they like, thanks to couponless discount offers.

Partnership agreements like these generate extra turnover. They also rejuvenate an established company's image where that image is too sedate. As Stacy Gratz, one of American Express's vice presidents puts it, the guiding principle is that people should think, "Wow, I wouldn't expect American Express to partner with this group."[2]

The connection between Lego and the Hollywood film industry is sixteen years old now. The powerful Danish corporation established links with Hollywood as early as 1999, when it signed a licensing agreement with the producers of *Star Wars*. A good dozen years later, the people at Lego devised and co-directed *The Lego Movie*. A Warner Bros. producer told *Bloomberg Businessweek*, "It's a hybrid movie made out of computer graphics and real bricks. They co-built the movie."[3] In other words, Lego partnerships are not just mere collaboration. They are also about co-creation.

Tony Fadell spent years refining his skills at Apple before setting up his own company, Nest. Nest is redesigning the domestic appliances "we love to hate,"[4] as he says. It has made thermostats and smoke detectors into objects of beauty that blend harmoniously into people's interior design. Now like Allianz, Airbnb have decided to enter into a partnership with Nest. The agreement is based on the following observation: in North America, Airbnb hosts and guests belong to a generation that cares about the environment. Ninety-five percent recycle at least some waste.[5] They use much less energy than the national average. And so they are very happy to have "intelligent" thermostats, Nest's star product.

The technology in Nest's thermostats is state of the art. When you are ready to go home, Nest will set the temperature to your preferred level in time for your arrival. If you come in later than expected, it will make sure no energy is wasted. The interesting thing about Nest's partnership with Airbnb is that it incites property owners to rent via Airbnb rather than else-where. All the more important when every day sees a new competitor trying to break into the market.

# Quirky and General Electric

One partner has fewer than three hundred[6] employees, the other three hundred thousand.[7] Yet the partnership between Quirky and General Electric puts them on an equal footing. The two logos share equal billing on packaging.[8]

Quirky has an online community of some 900,000 do-it-yourself fans and inventors around the world who want to pool tips and advice. Every Thursday evening, users take a vote on all kinds of new ideas and schemes for "smart" home appliances. Quirky also manufactures domestic appliances, lamps and connected light-switches sold at Home Depot, Best Buy and at New York's Museum of Modern Art.

This California-based start-up and GE, the nation's most famous conglomerate, have joined up to raise the IQ of your home. They have launched Quirky+GE as a brand selling "smart" home products, including a sensor to monitor door opening and closing; a sensor to detect leaky plumbing; a sensor to control "smart" light bulbs. All of these can be ordered on your smartphone.

The Quirky+GE home page declares it to be "a partnership that will change invention forever."[9] More modestly, Beth Comstock, GE's president & CEO for business innovations, in a press release published in November 2014 stated that, "We have seen tremendous success working with Quirky and its community of inventors to find new ideas and bring them to market at remarkable speed."[10]

More interesting still is GE's bold decision to make thousands of its patents available on Quirky's platform, to help develop new technologies that will sustain the Internet of things[11]—a sector bound to prove extremely relevant to the future of a corporation known as the world's largest manufacturer of major appliances. Indeed, this is exactly why GE took the plunge, swapping a part of its intellectual property for the ingenuity and inventiveness of the people in the Quirky community.

We are seeing an increasing rise in the number of implausible partnerships. As well as showing how GE works with Quirky, I might have described other unlikely link-ups, such as Alibaba, the Chinese e-commerce giant, with Lending Club. Lending Club is the world's biggest peer-to-peer lending system, which now offers small American businesses very cheap loans to buy Chinese-made products on Alibaba. Or Amazon and Twitter: Their partnership lets you add a product to your Amazon shopping list with just a click on Twitter. Or Transavia and eBay: When you enter a destination served by the airline, a "converter" suggests different items that the potential traveler could sell on eBay to raise the money for the ticket. Or Bosch and Henkel: These two big German companies have come up with "Wash and Coffee," cool coffee shops that are also Laundromats. The list goes on. . . . Up to Apple and Hermès who launched a watch in September 2015, beautified by the French luxury house. An improbable alliance between avant-garde technology and ancestral craftsmanship.

**Hence the questions:**

What if you partnered with a business as far removed from your own as possible?

And, inversely:

What if you linked up with a company operating in the same sector as you?

# 15

# Brand-Led Disruption

"Think Different." Very few slogans encapsulate what a company stands for in such a compelling way. Our agency in Los Angeles, TBWA/Chiat/Day, came up with it in 1997 to mark Steve Jobs' return. He had no new products to sell. The spirit of Apple needed urgent revival. Lee Clow, our network's creative leader, puts it this way: "We had to reach back and find the soul of the company once again."

Steve Jobs loved our two-word motto, convinced, as he was, that "people with passion can change the world for the better."[1] He regarded the film we made showing Einstein, Picasso, Gandhi, and many other guiding spirits as "honoring the people who think different and move the world forward." The impact of "Think Different" was not just external. The internal resonance was important too. Our posters showing twentieth-century geniuses stayed on the walls at Apple for years, in the reception area and elsewhere. I imagine they made a tiny contribution to people's hunger for innovation as they passed them every morning on their way to work.

In a book published in 2007 called *How Disruption Brought Order*,[2] I tried to depict how advertising works at its best. When client chief executives quote our slogans in their speeches, we know we've hit the right spot.

Steve Jobs referred to "Think Different" when he addressed IT retailers. Erich Stamminger, the former CEO of Adidas, exclaimed "Impossible Is Nothing" before a crowd of enthusiastic employees.[3] Carlos Ghosn has quoted the word "Shift" in motor shows in Tokyo and in Detroit.

All three of these company chief executives were using words from advertisements to communicate their visions of their corporations. Not that we had invented anything. All we did was to express what their companies stand for. Our skill lies in the ability to encapsulate concepts in two or three words. This way, a company's vision of itself acquires renewed strength and unsuspected authority. In this form, vision becomes meaningful. It informs a company's many different spheres of activity, including the most important of all: innovation.

In their own way, as slogans, "Think Different," "Shift," and "Impossible Is Nothing" made a contribution to innovation. Indirect, intangible but real.

## Tesco: Every Little Helps

Such slogans have a sell-by date. Firms tire of them. They come to want new ways of expressing what they stand for. Probably, they are wrong in this. But at least a good slogan serves as a catalyst as long as it lasts; it acts as an energy booster.

"Every Little Helps" survived longer than most. For nearly twenty years, British customers could not think of Tesco without these three words entering their heads. They captured the spirit of the brand to perfection. Today this is remembered as "the most ingeniously humble slogan ever written."[4]

Initially "Every Little Helps" referred to what the company was doing in terms of pricing, product range, services. Soon however the phrase extended its meaning beyond what had already been achieved to become a source of inspiration, a starting point for new ideas. Every Tesco employee came to develop a Japanese-type mentality. She or he would think: What can I do to help my company improve its offer? To try to come up with the next new idea to improve client experience. Tesco's management even set up a bonus system to reward employees whose suggestions were taken up.

I know that Tesco is going through tough times now, but back then the company was a pioneer in a whole raft of little things. Its range of organic, low-fat products was the broadest. It established a line of healthy infant meals. It was the first firm to give children their own little shopping carts. Its customer loyalty card, "Clubcard," was so well conceived that it enabled Tesco to develop a database containing information on some thirty-eight million shoppers worldwide.[5]

"Every Little Helps" started out as a slogan. But it became the motto that embodied everything the brand stood for.

## Marriott: Travel Brilliantly

A strong brand idea makes a brand magnetic. And as far as innovation is concerned, a strong brand idea has twofold strength. On the one hand, there's the notoriety, the good reputation, which ensures everything the brand creates is known immediately. On the other hand, there's the Tesco effect, where a strong brand idea becomes a launch pad for innovation.

"Travel Brilliantly" is the perfect example. After all, innovation hardly springs to mind when it comes to hotels. People might think of comfort, restfulness, a warm welcome: services that may be new but are not, strictly-speaking, innovative. With "Travel Brilliantly," Marriott has given itself a slogan that forces it to implement ideas that take it off the beaten track. Which is maybe why *Forbes* magazine designated Marriott as the most innovative brand in its sector in 2014.[6]

"Get teleported into your first-ever virtual travel experience,"[7] says Marriott. Its Oculus Rift Teleport system catapults you into a different world the minute you don its headphones and goggles. "The fully immersive, 4-D virtual journey transports you from Big Ben to Maui right from our lobby," the company adds.[8] Of course virtual reality drives reality. By giving us a foretaste, Marriott makes us want to travel for real.

Marriott has "brilliantly" redesigned its lobby experience. It has set up a social network called "Six Degrees," embodied both as an app and as an interactive tablet in hotel lobbies and currently under trial at Boston's Marriott Cambridge. Six Degrees acts in conjunction with LinkedIn to let clients know who else in the hotel shares their interests.[9] Staff are also able to map clients by affinity and organize relevant activities, such as wine tastings. The range of functions is pretty astonishing. When clients place their mobile phones on one of the lobby tables, for instance, a LED path will appear to connect them according to mutual spheres of interest.

"Travel Brilliantly" builds Marriott's chosen brand vision to innovate the future of travel. It is a concise formula that defines an ambition and captures the company's vision in two words, as well as giving it a new lease of life. The slogan's effectiveness can be measured in the way it has radically changed how the people at Marriott see their own company. They don't just think of themselves as working for a prosperous hotel chain: they see themselves as working for a company with a sparkling future. A simple, well-judged slogan can really make staff commitment blossom.

## Zappos: Happiness Management

You have been hired for a one-month trial period. Your boss wants you to stay. But he offers you good money to leave. What is this? It is the Zappos approach. Zappos expects every single member of staff to be totally committed to its culture. Offering someone two thousand dollars to leave after only one week on the job is an unexpected way of testing that commitment.

"Powered by Service" sums up the Zappos spirit: this is a brand obsessed with only one thing, improving customer service. As far as that is concerned, anything goes. For instance, a call-center employee sent a customer flowers after she had returned a pair of shoes bought for her husband, who died in a car crash. Staff at Zappos call centers are not given formulas as to how to respond. Customer phone time is unlimited. Wikipedia claims Zappos' longest phone call lasted precisely ten hours and twenty-nine minutes. . . .[10]

The company's single-minded insistence on offering the best-ever customer experience has a corollary. This second goal can be seen as a cause and consequence of the first: Zappos wants its employees to be happy. Tony Hsieh, Zappos' cofounder and chief executive officer, is convinced happy employees put everything they have got into giving their customers maximum satisfaction. And he is ready to bet that this policy will bring its rewards. A stream of new schemes, events, and training programs aim to spread felicity across the company. "Happiness management," as he calls it. Indeed, he has written a book, published in 2011, called *Delivering Happiness*.[11]

To anyone who thinks this is over the top, I would say that the people at Zappos are its premier ambassadors. On social media especially. Less than ten years after the firm was set up, it has reached number twenty-three in *Fortune* magazine's "100 Best Companies to Work For" listings.[12] Having said this, being in the vanguard of managerial innovation is not always easy. Recently, some two hundred Zappos employees[13] resigned, unable to comprehend Tony Hsieh's latest experiments in self-management. Hsieh says there will be no change in policy. He still wants to "flatten out management hierarchies."[14] Zappos will continue as a no-title company.

Started in 1999, Zappos has now been bought by Amazon for $1.2 billion. Tony Hsieh sums up its success in these terms: "Your culture is your brand. Customer service should not be just a department, it should be the entire company."[15]

In each of these instances, Apple, Tesco, Marriott, Zappos, a brand acts both as a filter and as a source of inspiration: A filter, in that it eliminates any innovative ideas, however interesting, that fail to match the vision; and a source of inspiration, in that it stimulates the imagination and generates innovative ideas to nourish future business. In this sense, brands shape the future.

## Michelin: No Compromise

Michelin is the global leader in the tire market. Its guiding principle is an absolute respect for customers. Because the tire business is a safety business. This principle is the yardstick according to which products are designed and tested. Tire performance cannot, in a sense, be optimized in absolute terms. For example, road holding can be maximized either for the long term or for the moment of purchase, but not both. Formula One racing illustrates this every Sunday during the season, with its high-performance tires that last only a dozen or so laps.

Car manufacturers are very mindful of how reporters will feel about their cars when they first test them. They want tires that work fabulously on their new models for those first few miles. But Michelin is convinced that what matters most is safety in the long term: a "no compromise" stance that drives the firm's innovation policy.

The manifestations of this are many. For instance, Michelin has always refused to make all-weather tires. Because drivers' winter requirements are too important. Offering medium-to-good road holding in summer and medium-to-good road holding in winter cannot, in Michelin's eyes, be the answer. Michelin has also refused to return to Formula One racing, because International Automobile Association specifications are conducive to developing tires whose technological advances cannot subsequently be transposed to meet drivers' everyday needs. Another example is that it is easy enough to manufacture tires that help reduce fuel consumption. The problem is that such tires are less durable. Again, Michelin will not compromise in this area. Its engineers are intent on designing low-friction tires to last.

So Michelin's overarching purpose is to optimize safety. Its key value is total moral integrity. Few companies are as successful at illustrating what A.G. Lafley, Procter & Gamble's CEO meant by, "Our purpose inspires us. Our values unite us."[16]

**Hence the questions:**

What if your company had a larger purpose than selling?

What if you chose a brand idea strong enough to foster innovation?

What if you started a bonus scheme to reward your employees' innovation ideas throughout the company?

# 16

# Insight-Driven Disruption

B ill Bernbach was the most famous adman in the last century. He always said, "Nothing is more powerful than an insight to build on."

Insights are tiny details stolen from people's lives, little intrusions into their ways of thinking and behavior; little remarks that may betray commonly held feelings. Such as this ad headline in the form of a question, "Have you reached that age when your boss is younger than you are?" If you have reached that age, this ad will draw your attention. You will stop and read it. Insights reinforce impact.

Insight is so fertile and so inspiring a concept that many definitions exist. James Hurman, a great planner from New Zealand, gives a few of his colleagues'.[1] To some, insight is a new point of view immediately recognizable. Many young athletes have been led to believe that what they wear—their jerseys, their caps, their sneakers—will make all the difference. As if that was all it took to make them win. Gatorade believes the opposite, that athletic performance is driven from the inside, hence the advertising claim: "Gatorade, Win from Within." "In" counts for more than "on," such is the insight.

Others regard insight as the underlying reason behind whatever is happening. Knowing that it costs infinitely more to win over new customers than to retain existing ones, Sainsbury's has spent years trying to get customers to spend more when they go shopping. Hence their famous and highly effective slogan: "Try Something New Today."[2] This arose out of an observation from AMV BDDO planner Craig Mawdsley when he accompanied shoppers on their outings. He saw that they "sleep-shopped," or, as he puts it, that "One shopper could wheel her trolley around, maintain conversation and eye-contact with me, whilst pulling items off the shelf over her other shoulder without even looking. She knew her routine so well."[3] This led Sainsbury's to break British customers' repetitive routines and suggest buying a new product every time they stepped into a store. From one single observation, Sainsbury's was able to increase annual sales by £2.6 billion.[4]

Still others believe that insight is about grasping the hidden nature of things. This is exactly what we did when we produced a campaign for Sony's PlayStation, which we called "Double Life." Some video gamers spent most of their lives enjoying their favorite pastime. It is almost as though—this is the insight—they only truly feel alive when sitting down in front of a console. Gamers, in other words, lead two distinct lives: ordinary, everyday life and the life they create when they plunge into a game. The hidden truth is that with PlayStation people do indeed lead a double life.

James Hurnam also quoted an English Planner who said, not without malice, "Insights are things that other people think of, that you immediately wish you had."[5] That was exactly what I felt on discovering, a few years back, the Dove campaign that showed us how beautiful all women are. The campaign was an ode to different shapes and sizes, a hymn to self-confidence. A film called *Camera Shy* showed us one woman after another one turning her head aside or putting her hands up in front of the camera to avoid the lens. Then a sentence appears on the screen: "When did you stop thinking you are beautiful?" Immediately after, some little girls of the sort that believe they are princesses come up. The truth is that all little girls feel like princesses. Until one day they grow into young women. When an ad captures this sort of insight and is able to display such deep understanding of the way individuals feel, then it becomes timeless. Never mind whether the campaign was created yesterday or twenty years ago, or whether it is going to be seen in twenty years' time. Dove's Camera Shy commercial perfectly illustrates this.

Procter & Gamble has its own definition of insight. "It is a discovery about the consumer that elicits an emotional reaction along the lines of 'you obviously understand me.'"[6] In this sense, insight is not just the basis of engaging campaigns. Insight is much more than this. It is a source of inspiration for new products. And innovation.

In his book *The Game Changer*,[7] A.G. Lafley gives many examples to show the importance of identifying insights and observing people in minute detail. In Mexico, for example, Procter & Gamble brought out a laundry detergent that did not really foam much. The trouble was, Mexicans regard foam as a sign of effectiveness. In the same market, P&G almost launched a classic softener, which demands two rinses. Now this would not have worked, because Mexicans want to save as much water as they can. So P&G came up with a new formula for softeners, requiring only one rinse. Now local consumers feel that this foreign company does "understand them."

## L'Oréal: Beauty Rituals

In the beauty sector, L'Oréal is the only major pure player in the world. The company regards beauty as a voyage of discovery, a scientific journey of exploration.[8] The people at L'Oréal are always looking into the scientific origin of cosmetic problems. This is not just applied science in the usual sense: L'Oréal plays a key role in fundamental dermatological research programs and skin sciences.

More precisely, as global scientific director, Jacques Leclaire, told me, L'Oréal has established research programs in bioengineering. The aim is to use progress in genetics and stem-cell technology to create new molecules. Whether discovered randomly or by intention, these compounds have generated a growing interest in bio-reactant molecules (molecules made from living beings) as opposed to standard compound chemistry, which is a cross-fertilization of chemistry with physics and mathematics. Every major advance in health care in the last three decades has stemmed from biology.

Skin is the focal point of all the science L'Oréal engages in to develop products. From research into the way skin reproduces itself by means of stem cells; into the factors that help skin stay young; and discovering how skin can be made to grow, to renew itself in order to delay aging. Clearly, bioengineering will occupy an increasingly fundamental, not to say central, role in any procedure intended to help understand the physiology of human skin and its pathologies. By establishing partnerships between its own laboratories and other specialized academic entities, L'Oréal has ensured that it holds a leading role in this field.

An interesting element is that L'Oréal's advanced scientific focus comes with an equally advanced approach to marketing. As Laurent Attal, L'Oréal's executive vice president for research and innovation, puts it, "We foster the constant interaction between marketing and research because we believe that the big ideas come from these interactions."[9]

L'Oréal's marketing focuses a lot on observation. Customer behavior is studied according to ethnic background, age, food habits and geographic or cultural circumstances. The marketing departments at L'Oréal know that Japanese women will brush their eyelashes up to one hundred times when applying mascara and that skin translucency is considered to be the absolute yardstick against which beauty is measured in their country. They know that Chinese hairdressers will spend three-quarters of an hour shampooing their customers' hair because, really, they are providing a massage service; that Brazilian women with very dark skin are not interested in lightening their complexions, only in reducing imperfections; and that Indians use talcum powder on their faces every day for a matte effect. Each of these observations stimulates innovation—and sometimes disruption—in L'Oréal's product range. They even have a name for this body of knowledge: geo-cosmetics.

There is no end to how well a corporation needs to know its customers. The next step for L'Oréal is to discover why a given product may suit some people and not others in identical circumstances. Answering this question will afford ever more detailed customer "clusterization," and even more specific product customization. Until a point is reached when the offer is individualized.

Which will be the epitome of the power of insights.

## Big Bazaar: Chaos on Purpose

Let us now proceed from the impeccable world of L'Oréal to the chaos of the Indian retailer Big Bazaar. Strolling around the aisles of a Big Bazaar store, all sorts of heady, spicy odors waft over one. Bright colors blossom everywhere. Products spill out of containers placed on the floor. People bump into each other. The senses come alive. Here lies life itself.

So welcome to the wonderful world of India's pioneer supermarket brand, employing around 35,000[10] people at 214 stores.[11] Everything may seem utterly haphazard, but really it is planned down to the finest detail. There is nothing fortuitous about Big Bazaar. No place for improvisation.

Big Bazaar's founder, Kishore Biyani experienced resounding failure when he tried to import the Tesco/Walmart model into India: all those long, clean aisles, those well-ordered shelves in stereotyped stores with air-conditioning, clear graphics and staff trained in Western sales techniques. Against all expectations and contrary to what the international management consultants were saying, Indian customers felt these supermarkets were not meant for them. The very basics of retail success in developed economies proved counterproductive in India. The immaculate tiling worried Indian consumers. To them, it meant that the goods on display were not going to be cheap.

So Kishore Biyani turned to street markets and their ancestral habits. He decided to make these viable on a large scale. By definition a street market is local. Big Bazaar had to be local too: local traditions are particularly important in India and this shows in the product range. At Big Bazaar, goods are displayed in bulk, in big sacks, where customers can help themselves. Bananas are sold in supermarket carts, as they are by the roadside. Every week, a "Wednesday Bazaar"[12] is organized, a day of special offers, at rates reduced beyond anything people could imagine in the West. At Big Bazaar, Indian consumers bargain for goods as they might at a street-stall. And when they've settled a deal, an army of employees is there to help them peel and chop the vegetables they've purchased.

Kishore Biyani decided to put himself in the shoes of what he calls the "serving class,"[13] meaning the future middle class. As a consequence, his stores welcome some three hundred million customers a year.[14]

The interesting thing with insights lies in that, as soon as they are discovered, they seem blindingly obvious. Although, evidently, somebody had to think of them in the first place. In this case, somebody had to have the guts to go against habits tried and tested the world over.

For Kishore Biyani, chaos was the insight. "We cannot survive in cleaner environments," he says. "We can only survive in chaotic environments."[15]

## Netflix: Knowing Customers Better than They Know Themselves

Back to the West and Netflix, the company that has invented algorithms to tell you what movie or series you want to watch, before you know it yourself. As an online streaming media company, Netflix is aware of every single thing you watch and every single thing you no longer want to watch. It knows what equipment you use, whether tablet, phone or TV. It knows what you share on social networks; what day, what time and in what place you watch your programs. Needless to say, it knows what season and what episode in that season you've reached. Nothing escapes Netflix, not even when you go back to see something you've seen before.

Netflix's algorithm is now a skillful blend of many algorithms. The company has also devised some of the most sophisticated tools in the world for data visualization, which bring up aspects of data that would otherwise be invisible. In this way, Netflix garners a million insights much faster than it otherwise would. Consequently, Netflix improves the suggestions it offers each user.

Less well known is the fact that Netflix's algorithms also determine what programs get produced and which actors get cast. According to Zach Bulygo,[16] one of KISSmetrics's bloggers, before green-lighting *House of Cards*, Netflix had assessed the number of its customers that had seen David Fincher's most recent picture, *The Social Network*, from start to finish. They also knew the ratings for the British version of *House of Cards* and the percentage of their subscribers who had seen Kevin Spacey or David Fincher movies. So production decisions are taken on the basis of extraordinarily specific data. Netflix even went so far as to produce ten different trailers for the series, each one appealing to the specific tastes of one section of the potential audience.

Netflix "wants to become HBO faster than HBO can become Netflix"[17] according to its bosses. And Netflix will achieve this goal for the simple reason that it has access to thousands and thousands of insights that HBO doesn't. HBO is monolithic. Whereas, "there are 33 million different versions of Netflix,"[18] told the company's Vice President Joris Evers to the *New York Times*.

Like Amazon or Uber, Netflix has acquired an incredibly insightful knowledge of its audience. It can thank big data for this. It can thank its analysts and the precision of its algorithms too. But in many other sectors of the economy, interpreting data is not always a mathematical exercise. Sometimes, all you need is to follow your intuition, to determine which bit of information matters most.

## SNCF: The Opinion Paradox

SNCF, the French National Railway Company, harvests tons of data every day, captured at national, regional, and local levels. Given the sheer quantity of information, this data is extremely hard to read. But it does enable SNCF to know more or less where it stands in the eyes of its public in real time. The truth is that SNCF has a mixed reputation. On the one hand, it runs the best fast trains in the world. On the other hand, quality of service is uneven. There are strikes. There are weather problems. And often the TV news headlines are harsh. In short, SNCF's image is not what it should be.

At our agency, we had a thought, an intuition that we verified ad hoc. We asked arriving passengers just two questions, right on the platform. The first question was: "Was your trip satisfactory?" Ninety-two percent of passengers replied yes, regardless of whether they had been traveling on a suburban or a long-distance train. The clever thing was the second question. "Do you think that other passengers feel as positively as you do?" This time, 65 percent said no! That is a highly revealing and very inspiring insight. It helps us see things in an utterly new light. Individual opinions can be favorable even when public opinion is not. General media noise leads people to think that others are not satisfied even when they are. This finding led us to suggest that SNCF constantly monitor passenger opinion, in stations, on the Internet and anywhere else. Above all, we recommended that they publish the results in real time. In our view, this is the best and probably only way to solve the opinion paradox. Every single person needs to become aware of other people's satisfaction.

Netflix's data scientists, L'Oréal's marketing specialists and the people at TBWA are all trying, in their own way, to do the same thing. They are turning data into knowledge. And knowledge into insights.

**Hence the questions:**

What if you took clusterization all the way to individualization?

What if you created a specific team to turn facts into knowledge and knowledge into insights?

What if you considered doing just the opposite of what strategy consultants usually recommend?

# 17

# Business Model Disruption

How about opening a bank account at the local tobacconist? Who would have thought of that? Nowadays, though, such things seem almost natural. The most astounding commercial ideas abound. Companies leap from one market to the next. Cautious, old-fashioned diversification, with its notions of adjacency and broadening product ranges, has gone the way of all things. Vertical development strategies (like Delta Air Lines buying a Pennsylvania oil refinery) and horizontal ones (like Pepsi taking over Gatorade) are no longer at the forefront of discussion. In fact, words like "vertical" and "horizontal" do not really have a place in today's business jargon. People are innovating and diversifying all over the shop. Uber is pondering its next move. Will it become a grocery supplier? A postal service provider? Or a catering deliverer? Toms, of course, has gone from selling shoes to growing coffee.

Opening a bank account at the local tobacconist's is something now possible with Nickel in France.[1] You can transfer money, arrange direct debits, deposit cash, and pay over the counter in 28 million outlets, spread through 215 countries, as well as making online payments and using ATMs . . . all for 20 euros per year.

This business model is different from normal banks' in several ways. There is no screening: anyone can have an account. There are no forms to fill out. All fees are inclusive, even the cost of setting up an account. Depositors' savings are not placed on the money markets.

Overdrafts are not allowed. This restriction has the advantage that people cannot go wild and start the month in the red. So holders of the Compte-Nickel do not have to pay interest on an overdraft. The account was originally designed for low-income customers, who still constitute some 75 percent[2] of its clientele and for whom those excessive fees amount, on average, to half a month's salary per year. The other 25 percent[3] of Nickel's customer base is more comfortably off and often travels abroad. No commission is charged on exchange rates.

To question conventional wisdom is the starting point for new business models. Apple, Nespresso, Tesla, Airbnb . . . today's new companies have chosen the disruption model. They have deliberately gone against what was done before. Which is why the term *disruption* has become so successful. At the time, when we decided to remodel it, it was a provocative way to describe what bold companies were doing when they chose radical innovation over incremental progress.

Most of the business stories I have touched on in this book are based on business models in which at least one major element is radically altered. Xiaomi sells only over the Internet, Lego lets customers design products, Big Bazaar has reinvented the street market. Burberry wants online experience to inspire the products it offers. Haier is structured around four thousand self-managing units. Spotify has put a limit to free streaming time . . . Breakthrough decisions such as these have a domino effect on all other parts of the business model, which change accordingly. Sometimes—Apple is the pioneer here—the entire model is disruptive.

## Apple: Leveraging Third-Party Assets

Apple has offered the most revolutionary products of the last decade. It has also invented a new business model in which all the parts relate to every other part. Apple has put in place a brilliant system in which interactions prosper and thrive: from products to stores, from iPod to Mac, from iTunes downloads to iPad subscriptions.

The magic of this business model is that it has become a platform to leverage third-party assets: a platform for other businesses to build on. The App store and iTunes allow app developers to earn millions of dollars through their transactions, which in turn consolidate Apple's business. As Henry Chesbrough points out in *Open Services Innovation*, "The crowning achievement of a business model is that it attracts external companies (or contributors) to invest in business activities that embrace the value of the platform."[4]

Everything reinforces everything else. The iPad sold well because it was supported by the App Store. This website has always had the best offer in terms of software applications and remains the one where their designers want to publish first. But the App Store would never have been so successful if it was not in turn based on the iTunes story. And iTunes was originally established to boost iPod sales. Now it promotes TV series, movies, books, and games. Apple has established an ecosystem, leaving other companies still struggling to sell marginally improved bits of hardware.

Apple's model feeds itself. Companies make products and services for Apple, which Apple will deliver through its platforms. Other companies develop applications for iPhone and iPad usage. Henry Chesbrough says, in the same book that "others are investing money that will help Apple make more money."[5]

This practice is just one aspect of Apple's business model. It is central to Facebook, because Facebook's worth is rooted, not only in the value of its platform, but also in the content that its users constantly generate. There are over 1.49 billion Facebook users worldwide.[6] That is over 1.49 billion people who work for Facebook for free. Amazon, in the same spirit, has opened its platform to other companies in order for them to sell their products. The result is that Amazon obtains a whole range of data at no cost, which will make its website more attractive and more efficient over time.

Businesses now compete by establishing new business models, which are harder to copy than products. In other words, business models have become a protection and a competitive edge of a new sort. Apple and Facebook have proven that putting others to work within their business models prevents those business models from being copied.

## Tesla: Stored Sunlight

Tesla's electric car boasts one of the most disruptive business models in the world.

The product is everything. Elon Musk, Tesla's founder, refuses to see electric cars as a version of internal combustion–engine cars. As far as he is concerned, the only way to achieve widespread adoption is to design the best car, regardless of power source. Performance, speed, and security have to be of the highest. Seventy to eighty percent of the Tesla car is designed and made in-house.[7] Most car manufacturers use a lot more sub-contracting than that. More and more they tend to assemble parts made by other people. Tesla's approach offers better quality control and better profitability.

Tesla cars are configured and ordered online, whether at a Tesla outlet or at home. Customers can follow the manufacturing process right down to delivery. The company sends its cars software updates designed to constantly improve driving pleasure. Software is getting so sophisticated that within a few years, Tesla, too, will be sending out driverless cars.

Doing without a dealership network is the most disruptive part of the Tesla model. Gone is the interminable haggling with dealers, the unverifiable repair bills. Tesla points of sale are not located where car dealerships are usually located. Tesla cars are sold in malls or near rail stations, places where people naturally aggregate; where potential customers feel much more relaxed than in remote warehousing districts. In fact, every single aspect of Tesla's model is disruptive. Nothing is designed or made the way conventional automakers design and make things. Tesla has built itself an innovative ecosystem of its own.

On April 30, 2015, in Los Angeles, Musk introduced Tesla Energy.[8] His presentation was remarkable. The new product is an instance of highly disruptive technology, with exponential potential for growth. So what was it all about? Solar-powered batteries to hang on a wall in someone's apartment or in a manufacturing plant. The batteries themselves are elegant, almost beautiful, and come in every shade. When several of them are hung side by side, they form a "Powerwall" or, if the wall is gigantic enough, what Elon Musk calls "Powerpacks."

Clearly, it would take hundreds of millions of these batteries for the planet as a whole to convert to sustainable energy. But as Musk says, "aren't we making a hundred million cars and trucks every year? Shouldn't we be rushing to build the same number of

Powerpacks?" Tesla wants to. And in order to get there, it is publishing its technical specifications and charts for free, so that companies wishing to join its colossally ambitious scheme can develop their own "Gigafactories."

This is a revolution in the offing. The main obstacle to widespread usage of solar energy is the question of storage: we need to be able to generate power by day and store it by night. If we did, we would soon find ourselves shifting to a zero-carbon electricity situation. And that would be a blessing to those remote corners of our planet, where the power supply is intermittent, expensive or nonexistent.

Elon Musk calls his dream "stored sunlight."[9] It is, he says, the only foreseeable path, the only way for mankind and all our fellow creatures on this planet to stay around. He is an incomparable salesman.

## Alibaba: The Ultimate Ecosystem

The biggest business ecosystem in the world's second-largest economy is called Alibaba. According to *Fortune* magazine, "this is an e-commerce colossus that is roughly the equivalent of eBay, PayPal, and Amazon combined."[10] Jack Ma, a former English teacher, first encountered the Internet in the mid-nineties. He realized immediately that the World Wide Web would transform China beyond recognition. Four years later, in 1999, he launched Alibaba, a wholesale platform designed "to make it easy to do business anywhere."[11] In truth, what Ma did was to open a virtual-reality marketplace, long before Chinese e-commerce took off. The man was not an engineer but he became one of his nation's Internet pioneers. He was not primarily interested in technology; he was first and foremost concerned about his clients' needs. Which is why he managed to make the basics of e-commerce comprehensible to millions of Chinese craftsmen and small manufacturers, whose lives were utterly transformed by his offer.

Three-quarters of all electronic transactions in China run through Alibaba.[12] By comparison, Rakuten, the top Japanese site, controls less than 30 percent[13] of its domestic market. Behind this achievement lie colossal logistical power and the ability to deliver six billion parcels per year—more than UPS's worldwide workload.

In 2004, in order to reassure Chinese customers, who are often wary of making online payments prior to receiving goods, and to satisfy sellers, who need to make sure that their customers are solvent before shipment, Jack Ma launched his own payments system called Alipay. Alipay blocks money for payment with a reliable third party during the delivery process. It has played a crucial part in Chinese consumers' ability to switch to e-commerce, because many are without bank accounts. Today, Alipay is the most successful payments system in the country.

"We are an Internet company that happens to be in China,"[14] Alibaba's founder once said, in an interview with Charlie Rose. "My vision is, if we can help Norwegian small businesses sell things to Argentina and consumers from Argentina buy things online from Switzerland, we can build up what I call . . . the e-WTO."[15] Facilitating goods transactions around the world has become Ma's obsession.

One platform is not enough. From the start, he has chosen to diversify the range of his activities, starting with a person-to-person e-commerce platform called Taobao, the number-one website through which 90 percent[16] of Chinese e-transactions are conducted. He then launched Tmall.com, a virtual mall that includes many major international distributors. Now Bloomingdale's, Macy's, Saks Fifth Avenue, and Ann Taylor have all signed up for Alipay.[17]

"eBay may be a shark in the ocean," says Jack Ma, "but I'm a crocodile in the Yangtze River. If we fight in the ocean, we lose—but if we fight in the river, we win."[18] Well, the crocodile is doing just fine. In 2014, Alibaba raised more than $25 billion on Wall Street, the biggest stock-market IPO of all time. And the market will continue to support Alibaba. According to Forrester Research, cumulative online turnover for China alone will be above a trillion dollars by 2019.[19]

## Airbnb: A World Without Strangers

In the business-to-business field, leasing has been replacing purchasing for years. Xerox, for instance, now only bills its clients for printer and photocopier usage. It no longer sells them apparatus. In effect, it manages a fleet of machines and only charges fees for upkeep and maintenance. Recently, it has taken this service concept even further, by agreeing to look after photocopiers and printers purchased from rival manufacturers.

In other words, Xerox clients' fixed costs have been transformed into variable costs. And because Xerox clients no longer need to employ maintenance personnel, they save on overhead. In the process, Xerox has transformed one-off sales that may or may not be renewed into long-term subscriptions that are more naturally extended.

This, of course, is the Salesforce approach, which offers companies software by means of a web navigator, no longer as a product but as a service, in that only actual usage is charged on a pay-as-you-go basis. Access is more important than ownership. This is what peer-to-peer is all about. The sharing economy. Internet and social media make us want to exchange products and services rather than buy them, even though we may need to use a facilitating company. BlaBlaCar, Zipcar and Airbnb are good examples, all thriving in the two sectors where purchase prices are highest: cars and real estate.

Airbnb is now the world's biggest hotel chain. Unlike most Internet companies, such as Google and Facebook, which earn their money off ads, Airbnb's income is derived from real transactions with customers. As it happens, Airbnb works with our agency in Los Angeles. I'd like to go into Airbnb's model, which is unique in many ways, in a little more detail.

Airbnb is a $25 billion company whose main asset is human hospitality. Despite having more than one million potentially available rooms, Airbnb has few material assets: no factories, no production line, no physical product that it owns or manufactures. Its business relies on the simple act of people opening their door and welcoming in a stranger.

Airbnb has the ambition to be as universally recognized and understood as Apple, Nike, or Coca Cola. However, while these brands are built primarily by the company and projected out to the world, the Airbnb brand is the result of the passion and involvement of its community of more than twenty million people. Airbnb founder Brian Chesky often says there is no distinction between Airbnb employees and Airbnb's extended community. No wall between company and community. The community is the brand.

One obstacle to Airbnb's growth (apart from constantly changing legislation) is the idea that its model is weird. Welcoming someone you don't know into your home is weird. Staying with strangers is weird. Airbnb's 2015 communication focused on this issue, aiming to defuse the weirdness and undermine the very notion of "strangers." A campaign in January 2015 introduced the hashtag #nomorestrangers. A TV commercial aired in May started with the words "Dear Stranger." People realize that they can travel like locals and get a far more intimate experience of a city by staying in someone's private house. They can feel at home in any country in the world and realize that any stranger can easily be a friend.

The peer-to-peer economy is redefining the way in which products and services are created and exchanged. It has only been made possible by exponential progress in computer science. Information searches now cost next to nothing. Everyone can access in real time whatever is for sale or purchase, for hire or on loan. This makes products and services we use only occasionally much cheaper. So a wide range of new business models and start-ups can come into being. There is no limit to the possibilities.

Most companies like Amazon, Facebook or Alibaba that have entered the Fortune 500 since the year 2000 are based on disruptive models rather than on product innovation. Digital has been a catalyst to their business.

But more and more, digital is also an agent for change, bringing new energy to traditional business categories and established companies. Digital is forcing every single business leader in the world to rethink, sometimes to revolutionize, his or her company. Information technology is inspiring new business models in every sector, whether old or new.

One industry is stimulating imaginations in every other.

**Hence the questions:**

What if you sold a totally integrated ecosystem?

What if you created a peer-to-peer platform?

What if you transformed one-off sales into long-term subscriptions?

What if you had to face Google as a competitor?

# 18

# Anticipation-Driven Disruption

TBWA/Hakuhodo has shown itself to be incredibly good at leveraging collective intelligence.

The project, called Mirai Nihon,[1] was an extraordinary one. Our Japanese agency decided to design the first ever off-grid house in the world. Having the idea was not enough: we turned ourselves into an architecture firm, a real estate developer and project supervisor. We coordinated twenty different subcontractors and crowdsourced ideas from more than five hundred engineers and scientists.

# Mirai Nihon: The Future of Japan

The idea originated after the terrible tsunami that hit Japan in 2011. TBWA Tokyo's managing director was determined to make some kind of spectacular and concrete contribution to the country's new energy policy. Naturally, such a commitment extended far beyond his usual duties and field of expertise. And who could ever have imagined that one day an advertising agency would find itself collaborating on a daily basis with entities such as JAXA, the Japanese Aerospace Exploration Agency, to design a house? And then build it.

The tsunami swept away our Japanese employees' vision of the world they lived in. Suddenly, Japanese infrastructure systems seemed frail. Power could no longer be taken for granted. A decision was made that it would be good to design a house that would not be reliant on the usual power, gas, water, and telecom networks: a self-sufficient house, in which nature and technology would act together in mutual support. In order to achieve this goal, an inventory of all the related technologies and all the innovations yet to appear on the market was drawn up. Working relationships were established with Nissan Motors; with HEMS, the Home Energy Management System, a solar design lab; as well as with Cristal Valley Water Purification System and of course JAXA.

As far as this project was concerned, the Nissan Leaf, a 100 percent electric car, was not just a car, it was also an off-grid power generator, which, in tandem with solar energy, would be able to supply enough electricity for a standard-size home. Aero House, a mobile-home built of wood, was adapted to fit every recent technological advance. HEMS would allow homeowners to control energy consumption remotely with impressive precision. Cristal Valley would produce drinking water from the sea or from rivers, and decontaminate it if necessary. JAXA's contribution would come in the form of technologies designed for space-shuttle living. Each of our partners, working in conjunction with our Tokyo agency, was determined to innovate and make the most of new scientific discoveries.

Today, Mirai Nihon is no longer at the project stage. It exists in the form of a house by the sea, which sits on a wooded hill overlooking a quiet bay. "After taking responsibility for the energy I use," says the young Japanese woman who was the first to use the house, "I was reminded of my humble existence in nature."[2]

## Inventing Tomorrow

Building a self-sufficient home by means of crowdsourcing was TBWA's way of doing what it could to meet one of the crucial challenges of our time. Many other companies achieve this on a much larger scale, by launching initiatives that touch on a whole range of vital issues. Remember that *Time* magazine cover, "Can Google solve death?"[3] Google has hired more than one hundred world-renowned medical experts, who have been tasked with carrying out research on aging. The company has become the number one, private investor in health care issues.

Companies like Apple, IBM, Facebook, and Google are prone to invest in areas that have little to do with their core business, especially in areas likely to shape our collective future— such as education, energy, and health.

Apple, for example, invests massively in education. More than twenty thousand teaching apps are available on iPad. Most recently, it launched iBook 2, which makes schoolbooks interactive and offers dozens of teaching functions not to be found in classic textbooks. It is of course true that Apple is using this project to establish a leading position in what has become a massive market. And naturally, big publishers like McGraw-Hill and Pearson regard content creation as their home turf. Nevertheless, electronic textbooks' new technical capabilities are bound to influence, even determine, future editorial policy. Apple has even set up "The Apple Distinguished Educators Program"[4] to help support pioneering teachers and encourage them to become even more inventive and thus even more widely respected.

We live in the age of the MOOCs, those unbelievably successful, free, online college courses open to all. This is the knowledge revolution. Apple's decision to change the face of education by introducing radically new forms of textbook will make all the difference and fulfill one of Steve Jobs' great dreams. By rejuvenating schoolbooks, he wanted to contribute to the improvement of the American school system.

IBM is transforming energy consumption, water delivery, public safety, transportation systems, and emergency management by cross-referencing information mined from different data sources with tens of thousands of sensors placed in critical positions throughout a city. Its "Smarter Cities" program is teaching one hundred and twelve conurbations over five continents[5] to cope with the world's increasing urbanization. By 2050 two-thirds of the world's population are expected to live in cities. . . .[6] After the tsunami, the Japanese installed sensors in partially contaminated areas in Fukushima. This enabled IBM to map radioactivity across the country. It will help the authorities react faster in case of future catastrophe.

The interesting thing is how the "Smarter Cities" program came into being. In 2006, IBM organized a series of client and employee brainstorming sessions on innovation. The idea was not to increase turnover by means of its core business, but how best to use the energies and skills of its four hundred thousand employees to "make a better world." Indeed, "Smarter Cities" was originally a corporate social responsibility–driven project. The program operates on a vast scale, but initially there was nothing to suggest this might happen. Now IBM is looking ahead to issues that cities do not realize they will soon have to face.

When Facebook bought Oculus, it was not just looking at gaming, even though gaming is the main virtual-reality market. The Oculus Rift headset is much more than a portal into virtual reality. It is also a community of engineers aiming to develop thousands of applications for the Rift. They are working for architects, for students and doctors. Architects will be able to walk through buildings yet to be built and gauge their proportions. Students will be projected into a classroom situation, where they can learn history, geography, physics or chemistry in three dimensions. Future doctors will be able to travel down arteries to the heart and patients will talk to their doctors remotely. Virtual reality offers a wealth of possibilities, especially in the fields of physical therapy and psychiatry, preventing people from falling, helping them deal with pain, handling the after-effects of an accident or major stress.

Oculus is not just investing in education and health because there are major revenue streams to be found in those areas, but also because they are vital to our future. To this extent, Oculus is contributing to the CSR aspect of Facebook's business.

Google has decided to bet massively on health. Which is why it has set up a new company called Calico, which stands for the California Life Company. Calico has hired dozens of world-famous medical experts and set demanding goals, some of them, like finding a cure for cancer, potentially hugely significant. Google's two founders are heavily invested. They don't just want to improve life expectancy, they want to extend it dramatically. To this end, they have given Calico access to the gigantic mass of Google's databases, in the hope that it can identify the true causes of aging. Very little is known about how different parameters interact. Intelligently interpreted data may make a vital contribution to finding the answer.

What we do know is that caring for our internal organs will not suffice. We need to improve our understanding of tissue decay and what makes it happen. We also need to learn how to customize care and adapt it to match individual patient biomarkers.

As we have seen, new technology provokes revolutions across the board. This is especially true in the area that matters most to most people: health care. Google has made a strategic decision to stand far and above the rest in the technology/health crossover field. In this sense, a major private-sector player is giving itself a quasi-public mission.

For centuries now, around the world, all nations have counted on the public purse to fund costly, long-term projects such as roads, schools, and hospitals. At the same time, it is often said that companies are prey to short-term concerns and obsessed by quarterly results. But this is not always true, as we have seen. Some companies are showing that private-sector interests can partially compensate for diminishing public-sector budgets.

Google has focused on aging. Many other subjects of prime concern to our time, such as energy, education, and general health care, are attracting the attention of other large companies. Indeed, thousands of private companies around the world are doing what they can to enhance knowledge and work toward a better future.

In other words, the business world is picking up from where governments are tending to leave off, as they come to lack the two crucial resources that some private-sector companies now amply possess: time and money.

**Hence the questions:**

What if you decided to innovate in health, education and energy?

What if you deliberately affixed an out-of-reach goal to your company?

We have just gone through the Fifteen Innovation Paths that I personally feel to be the most eloquent. We have encountered many business stories along the way, that have thrown up a great number of What If questions. These can serve as a checklist before any meeting on innovation. You will find them listed in the back of the book.

It is worth forcing oneself to consider every question on its own terms. Many may initially seem incongruous or irrelevant to the brand or product under consideration. But perseverance will throw up unexpected connections and relationships. This is a great way to increase the prospect of innovation, to come up with something that might not otherwise see the light of day. The aim is to create a positive coincidence of a sort that cannot, normally speaking, be created: serendipity.

I recommend that every reader establish his or her own list of What Ifs, to add to ours, based on the case stories that have caught his or her imagination. The approach is totally open. Anyone can improve on or enrich it.

And if any single one of the What Ifs, or any of the Innovation Paths described above has stimulated a new thought, then this book will have served its purpose.

# PART

# THREE

# DISRUPTIVE BRAND BUILDING

Part One discussed the fact that companies can innovate at every different level. They can come with disruptive products, disruptive business models, disruptive marketing strategies, and disruptive communications plans.

Part Two described a variety of paths to stimulating innovation at the product and business-model levels.

Part Three is about marketing and communication. About everything related to brands. It defines what we call "disruptive brand building."

For several years now, the aggregate value of the S&P 500 companies' intangible assets has exceeded that of their tangible assets. Which means that patents, copyrights, registered trademarks, goodwill, client lists, company culture, training programs, and management systems are now worth more than physical factories and machines. And, most interestingly, among all the intangible assets a company may own, its brands are often the most valuable.

It follows that marketing is not just about selling products. It is also about creating added value in a company's most valuable asset. This is why it is essential to make sure that each brand vision is clearly defined and expressed in an ambitious way.

There can be no greater markcting sin than underleveraging a brand.

# CHAPTER
# 19

# Disruption Strategy

Disruption helps us find new growth for our clients by defining strategies for their brands, by breaking conventions that surround them and by building powerful visions.

The methodology, as we have said, falls into three parts.

It starts with Convention. These are the "box" we need to think out of. We try to identify all the things competitors are currently doing. We discover the accepted wisdom the consumer is stuck in. And we find the baggage in the brand's history that is holding it down. The status quo is something you need to understand completely, before you can think of challenging or overturning it.

Then you need a Vision, to steer a brand toward. Emerging cultural signals help us understand the world a brand inhabits. They show what trends you want to respond to and benefit from.

In order to break Convention, and to move toward our Vision, we need to conceive an idea that is as provocative as it can be. We call this "the Disruption." This is an original angle on the business that helps untie conventions it is trapped in and allow the brand to leap ahead of the competition.

Convention, Vision, and Disruption: taken together, these constitute our operating system. This is how we see the world. This is how we find growth.

## Imagining a Vision

In a world where markets and competitors are changing so fast, the role of Disruption has pivoted. It has become vital that companies and brands create a rallying point, a focal point and this despite the increasingly unsettled nature of the market—or rather because of it. We need to create a reference point to compare with constantly, whatever unexpected direction the market takes us in.

Also, communication channels have multiplied in so many different ways. Blogs, apps, social networks etc. offer a seemingly limitless range of communication choices. This multiplicity of choice leads to a risk of getting lost on the way, or scattering in all directions. Having a strong Vision can prevent from coming up with off-track initiatives.

For these two reasons, it is more crucial than ever to orchestrate everything around a clear and precise idea of what the brand stands for.

This is why the Disruption methodology, as a way of coming up with clear and engaging Visions, has never been so relevant. We have already discussed Gatorade. Soft drinks belong to a product category that is easy to imitate, yet, after trying for decades, the competition has not been able to erode Gatorade's dominance. Because the brand has a strong Vision. It believes that "athletic performance comes from within." The belief is not about electrolytes or hydration. It is about unlocking the power in each athlete. This is summed up in the campaign's theme: "Win From Within."

Already discussed was Airbnb, another TBWA client. Airbnb's game-changing Vision is to suggest we build a world "where strangers don't exist anymore." This is a very ambitious stance that goes way beyond the usual hospitality proposition, which focuses on service, amenities, comfort, and destination. Airbnb believes that the power of human hospitality opens up worlds. It is a powerful road map.

A third example of a great Vision is the Belgian bank, KBC. Its aim is to become a bank that benefits everyone, not only itself and its clients; a bank that sees itself as part of the fabric of society, not just a facilitator of transactions. The Disruption reads "Think of this bank as a public service." Some of the things they have done include having a call center staffed by seniors where people over 65 talk to 40-year-olds about retirement, as well as the "Gap in the Market" Web app that helps entrepreneurs explore business opportunities in Belgium and a "Room for Improvement" initiative, that enables business owners to better understand consumer needs and expectations . . .

Gatorade, Airbnb, KBC. Those are three great examples of Vision. Obviously, we have not changed the products. We have changed the perspective in which they are seen. Gatorade is not just a sports drink; it is a sports brand. Airbnb is more than just another hospitality network; it is an idea about what humans have in common. And KBC is more than a bank; it is a public service.

The need for strong Vision has always been central to our work. It has led to some pretty big brand ideas such as "Think Different," "Impossible Is Nothing," "Shift," "Win from Within" . . . But today's brands evolve in a digital world that makes owning a strong Vision even more essential. Digital is about everything being instantaneous. Digital accelerates everything it touches. Digital constantly renews the content it generates. Digital efficiency is measured in terms of the instant. By the number of clicks, the number of responses to every blog post and tweet. But advertising is about the trace it leaves. Its purpose is to structure the way people imagine brands and products. The basic principle is repetition, sedimentation.

So the more a brand digitizes its communication, the more opportunities are created to enter into conversations with specific audiences at any moment. But at the same time, digital communication fragments the messages. They become volatile. They leave a trace that is more diffused and less clearly defined.

This is one of the major challenges every brand must now face: articulating a multitude of messages, sent out to a highly fragmented audience, around a central, shared purpose and meaning. That central, shared purpose and meaning is what we mean by Vision.

Vision cannot be defined out of context. Devising a long-lasting Vision means understanding the changes that are underway in both culture and technology. Seemingly unconnected events may alter the landscape in crucial ways. We may need to defend our brands against such events. Or, better, to harness them creatively.

In this respect, we have developed three proprietary tools to help understand context: "Future Edging," "Business Hacking" and "Vision Composing." They reveal new consumer habits and business practices at the cutting-edge of popular culture.

We want to stretch our thinking, to embrace and adapt to radical future potentialities. We want to become "early adopters" of the future. And we are lucky enough to work with three companies that sit at the nexus where business, technology, and entertainment all meet: I mean Apple, Airbnb and Netflix.

I believe that this gives us an edge when it comes to making marketing work at the speed of popular culture.

We should never forget that brands that do not see the future coming usually do not have one.

## Hunting for Convention

The last sentence of the first Disruption book read: "Today's visions will be tomorrow's conventions." This has never been truer. Except that the time-frame has dramatically shrunk. From the moment an innovation appears on the market, the movement toward commoditization goes at a rate that has never been seen before.

We are now living in a world of fast emulators, copiers. Samsung could be the best example. The Korean company doesn't seem to have a visionary strategy, but a profitable business model, at least for a while. And on the heels of Samsung, other fast followers are already here, sometimes extremely powerful like Xiaomi, who plan to sell no less than 100 million smartphones in 2015. Actually, you could argue that Apple's entire innovation pattern is based on the idea of "opening and holding." As Apple creates new propositions and offers new attributes (touchscreen, app ecosystem, tablets, digital music . . .), it simultaneously needs to hold the market and prevent the competition from entering it as long as possible. Apple's legendary copyright lawsuits are there to prove it. Apple pays the price of being the innovator.

Airbnb is facing the same problem. Many of the things it has done that are revolutionary today will sooner or later become the new conventions in the marketplace. Over ten copycat sites already try to replicate what Airbnb does. Software development costs and the time required to generate software have been dramatically reduced, and users tend to gravitate toward new services and offers. One of the reasons why Apple and Airbnb succeed in containing new rivals and keeping one step ahead of the field is that they both have a strong vision and a business model in harmony with that vision.

Once again, digital makes the Disruption method even more relevant. Because digital accelerates the occurrence of conventions. Digital has disrupted the analog world. It has challenged many established business models. In this sense, it is often assumed that thinking digital means thinking disruptive. This is true when you compare digital with the analog world. But when we consider digital on its own, irrespective of the analog world, we see that the conventions it has spawned are numerous. In fact, the digital world is much more conventional than we think.

As far as business models go, the digital world tends to imitate Facebook, Apple, Google or Amazon. Not always wisely. In organizational terms, start-ups have brought disruptions in the form of campuses, labs, and horizontal management. But these ideas have become the new conventions. They are often painfully reiterated, parrot fashion, by corporations that are short on imagination. As to communication, all too often, digital sees people shifting analogue content over to the Internet without changing it in any way.

Again, this is why the Disruption methodology is so valid today. It can help overturn the conventional side of digital.

## Creating Disruption

When the Convention is identified and the Vision defined, the question is how do we move from one to the other. And do so in a fast, smart, unexpected way.

The answer is "by Disruption." Disruption is that little delta that changes a square to the circle. (This refers to the square, the circle and the triangle, the three symbols of our methodology). This is the one thing we really know how to do: make ideas for a radical new approach emerge from the friction between the Convention and the Vision.

The Disruption strategy is a statement that will act as an operating principle. This can be many different things. I'm again taking examples I previously mentioned in the book in order to highlight the approaches that underlie them. The statement can be a new *thought* such as when Gatorade explains that "in" is more important than "on," or a provocative *opinion*, such as when Airbnb says "Build a world without strangers." Or an *idea* unheard of, like when the KBC bank says it is going to act as a public service. It can also come in the form of an *initiative* never taken before, such as the "Adoption Drive" we recommended to Pedigree some years ago.

A Disruption Statement is what we "do against." So Disruption Statements matter. They really matter. They have to be good. They have to be media agnostic and hold true in the market over time. We cannot create against a Disruption that changes too often. This will seem erratic and produce uncertainty and just noise around the brand.

Anyone who has ever tried to come up with a disruptive brand strategy knows just how hard it is to find something sharp enough to create impact. And broad enough to carry a brand through an entire market cycle.

# CHAPTER
# 20

# Disruption Live

In the past, the Disruption methodology focused on strategy alone. Company and brand vision were designed to last for several years, so the need to call upon Disruption methodology did not arise often.

Today, opportunities for collaboration and exchange in real time have obviously grown exponentially. And, correspondingly, the practice of Disruption needed to embrace them. Disruption as a methodology had to become more agile. It had to become "snackable" and liquid.

"Snackable" because we need smaller formats and smaller forums to address the smaller questions that brands deal with on a regular basis. There can be Disruption in even small decisions. And liquid, because we have to accelerate, to move even faster—faster than the culture we all live in now. The practice of

Disruption had to turn into a flow. This is why we have developed new tools to make the methodology of Disruption truly real-time.

We have come up with what we call "Disruption Live" and reorganized our agency accordingly.

## The Open Brief

"Disruption Live" has led us to reconfigure ourselves to bring a brand to the world in real time. We monitor and respond to data, consumer insights and cultural stimulus. This ensures a high level of energy and a fast pace. It considers media thinking as an up-the-food-chain, strategic opportunity. "Disruption Live" says clearly what we think a modern agency model should be.

Of course, we have always been in the habit of offering clients proactive ideas to develop brand vision, ahead of the brief.

This, as an example, is a list of some of the ideas implemented for Adidas. In Tokyo, we devised something that CNN eventually came to call "Sky Soccer." In front of a miniature football field painted on a billboard on the roof of a building, soccer players, suspended from cables, played a game of vertical football. In New Zealand, we asked each player of the famous All Blacks national rugby team to give us drop of their blood. We then mixed this into the ink with which Adidas posters showing the team were printed, to the absolute delight and incredulity of fans. Close to Munich airport, a bridge was thrown over the highway in the shape of a goalkeeper's dive. So we had a 40-meter-high version of Oliver Kahn's body with cars speeding beneath. We also had a copy of the Sistine Chapel frescoes painted over the ceiling of the main railroad station in Cologne, with soccer stars in lieu of God and Adam. . . . The list of such initiatives and events is quite long. It fed the "Impossible Is Nothing" brand idea for Adidas and made that phrase ring true.

Such recommendations illustrate something we have always believed in. When a brand idea is strong, it inspires a great number of initiatives, which in turn make the idea even stronger. This is a virtuous circle. A brand is built over the long term through a series of short-term ideas.

But, in today's world, this is no longer enough. When it comes to online conversations, we cannot be satisfied with occasional initiatives. We need instant and constant engagement. The things that Adidas used to do from time to time to make its brand stronger now have to be conceived and implemented several times a day.

Real time is the new requirement.

The pace of work in-house has been completely overhauled. In organizational terms, our teams are now cross-functional, each one combining strategic planners, writers, art directors, social media specialists, data analysts, creative technologists, and so on. We have also settled on something that has become unavoidable today: a nine a.m. meeting, attended by everyone, every day.

These meetings are known as the Open Brief. Each day, new ideas are thrown into the ring for discussion. Teams analyze recent data findings to spot cultural and technological trends. Finally, Open Brief meetings are also where proprietary tools such as "Insight Mining" and "Connections Radar" are now used. What they do is pretty much self-explanatory.

The magnitude of each task determines the level of approval required for the ideas involved. Teams can green-light their own ideas up to a certain level. Larger briefs that require client input are set in a pre-defined presentation format and passed on for approval, thus unlocking a budget to finalize the creative and media proposal. Organizing things this way brings clients to establish a corresponding process to handle real-time input from agencies.

These methods shape our organization. They establish new ways of behaving. For instance, with a few of our brands, clients sometimes attend Open Brief meetings. Netflix is one example. And whenever clients do attend Open Brief meetings, they become an integral part of the brand group. Open Brief even affects our relationship with client legal departments. Creating content in real time implies not waiting three days to get legal clearance on a message.

To finish up on Open Brief, I would say that there is no "off switch" to Disruption. As Lee Clow, creative soul of our company, puts it, "Disruption is the active interpretation of the brand vision. It may have started as a noun, as a way of thinking, but it has become a verb. A thing we do. Every day."

## NURVE

NURVE is "Live Disruption" made real. "The Nissan United Real-time Vision for Engagement" is a platform[1] we conceived for Nissan Motors Limited.

Initially, this platform was based on the fact that social media have become indispensable to marketing. But soon, and this is the interesting thing, Nissan also came to notice that social media and the data it generates have a much broader operational benefit than just for marketing.

So Nissan asked us to turn a leading social media marketing operation into a fully-fledged, social business.

To achieve this, we designed a custom model built along the lines of Disruption Live. Part of this includes embedding NURVE personnel inside Nissan's headquarters in Yokohama. A key additional function is "Cross Business," which is a dedicated service to support non-marketing business units. Its core role is to work with the heads of each business unit within Nissan and explore ways NURVE can assist them in achieving their business objectives through the use of social business.

Another part of NURVE is generating content to feed our digital and always "on" world. It has to be specifically designed for social media and not just copying and pasting existing content from non-social media. Which is why NURVE has its own editorial capability, including editor-in-chief, writer, designer and motion artist. This small team produces more than 2,500 pieces of content a year, in partnership with Nissan.

Technology and particularly social technologies play a major role in the operation of NURVE. When the Periscope real-time video streaming service was launched in March 2015, an opportunity was created for Nissan. Nissan was one of the very first brands on the platform. New models were unveiled via a live-streaming event at the New York Auto Show only one week after Periscope was launched. Another example: a simple update on Facebook's newsfeed algorithm can have major consequences on how Facebook users behave. The NURVE team monitors these changes and defines the right course of action, which might be tweaking content strategy, finding a new social idea or even better, coming up with an innovation idea for the company.

As part of the "Cross Business" function, NURVE also supplies the Nissan human resources department with material to enhance their recruitment initiatives through LinkedIn. The content strategy for an audience of engineers is vastly different from that utilized to engage with consumers. Since NURVE started assisting Nissan with recruitment, more than 1,500 new employees have been hired via LinkedIn within twelve months.

Last but not least, an important part of NURVE is identifying online opinion leaders that Nissan can build relationships with. During calendar year 2014, relationships established with twenty or more highly influential individuals online have translated into reaching more than thirty million people, notably in the United States. To buy this level of influence through traditional marketing means would have required an investment of millions in media.

In short, NURVE delivers.


# SNCF LIVE

We gave ourselves a challenge: shooting a commercial in the afternoon, and broadcasting it on a major national channel the same evening, only a few hours later. Our client was SNCF, the French National Railway Company. The project: "SNCF Live."

Today SNCF, as I already mentioned, is one of the best railway companies in the world. But the corporation is currently in the throes of a major transformation. It has been modernizing its network for a number of years, which means asking passengers to show a high degree of understanding and adaptability. Yet, strikes and weather problems have come to constitute a systematic inconvenience that is morphing occasional bouts of passenger irritation into something more like widespread customer dissatisfaction.

In order to help passengers understand the extent to which SNCF is making efforts on their behalf, we devised and implemented Disruption Live. This is a gathering of strategic analysts, community managers, data analysts, creative executives and film crews located at the heart of the company. Every day, this unlikely team produces a film about all the changes that are afoot. The film is broadcast just a few hours later, prior to the main evening news program.

These films generate an impressive amount of chat on social networks. This in turn triggers content for real-time accounts of all the changes that are going on throughout the French railroad system.

At the time of writing, some forty-five films have been generated and broadcast over a period of forty-five days. They have been watched 252 million times on the TF1 television channel and website, and 22 million times on social networks. Our round-the-clock real-time unit has posted 4,933 messages live. As a consequence, more than 20 percent of the conversations about SNCF on Facebook and Twitter were around the campaign, with only 4 percent negative opinions occurring.

SNCF Live has brought us into direct, real-time contact with our client's clients. We will soon do something that has never been done before: commercials made in response to Twitter messages posted by SNCF clients that morning will be broadcast that same evening. When a classic broadcaster like TF1, moreover France's most viewed channel, joins the digital world in this way, then it is safe to say that Disruption Live is here to stay.

NURVE and SNCF Live are the way to go. This is where we should be heading with all our clients. Thinking on our feet in real time. Generating content day by day. It is a fundamental evolution of the Disruption methodology.

This is the future of disruptive marketing.

# Conclusion

This book has shown how Disruption® can help marketing executives in their quest for corporate growth.

Disruption Strategy offers them the prospect of a larger share of the future for their brands. Disruption Live provides the tools needed to place their company's quest for growth within the context of current popular culture. Disruption Paths can induce them to restore innovation to its rightful place at the heart of their activities.

In concluding, I would like to refer to three questions that often arise when we outline our method. What are the boundaries of Disruption? What part has Disruption played in our TBWA culture? And how does Disruption help chart a course through the increasingly complex maze that the world has become?

Initially, Disruption was designed for advertising. Then it became a catalyst for business as a whole. We now know it can jump-start change inside companies. In this sense, it is related to other problem-solving techniques.

The classic Convention-Vision-Disruption sequence has proven effective beyond its original communications function. It has stimulated innovation in fields as diverse as the search for new retail distribution networks, R&D prioritization, diversification policies, reorganizing HR, developing investment analyst presentations and the establishment of a common culture in newly merged companies.

We have organized Disruption Days for national governments in Finland and Thailand. In both these countries, and clearly for quite different reasons, the authorities needed to rejuvenate their industrial policies. At a completely different level, we even organized Disruption Days for philanthropic organizations and for a leading law firm.

Disruption has changed the way we work on a daily basis. The method and its spirit are what makes our agency different. Over time, we have come to forge the language of Disruption with its own vocabulary. No other agency speaks of Convention, Disruption, Media Arts, Business Hacking, Vision Composing, and so on. All these proprietary concepts are essential to our way of thinking.

Bill Taylor is the founder of *Fast Company*, a magazine that ranks the most innovative companies in the world on a regular basis. He says that the most successful ones use their own original words to describe what they do because their thinking is different.[1] They devise their own language and this sets them apart from their rivals. "Their vocabulary," he adds, "is what they see as an in-house jargon that illustrates how they like to enter the fray, how they like to work, how they want to succeed and what winning means to them."

My last point is about simplicity. Some people feel that Disruption is complicated. It is not. It is about starting out thinking deeply and then coming up with something simple. We have enriched the method with a range of tools and exercises. We need that common ground, a base to start from. It may look mildly prescriptive. But it is not. Rigid thinking is to be shunned. Disruption is not a system. It is a source of inspiration.

As Sir Jonathan Ive, Apple's chief design officer, says: "Simplicity is not simple."[2]

Well, providing simplicity is what Disruption does. As a method, Disruption is based on a strikingly simple road map: Convention-Vision-Disruption. That sequence remains as fertile as it ever was. In today's world:

Complexity has become the Convention.

And Disruption brings simplicity.

# Disruption What Ifs

*Open*

What if consumers were to become your own R&D department? Or your sales force?

What if you created from scratch an online community dedicated to innovation?

What if launching imperfect products were the best way to innovate?

*Structural*

What if you used the minimum viable product (MVP) strategy?

What if you gave a limited time frame to all your innovation projects?

What if you created a lab or a Fab Lab?

*Asset*

What if your core asset became the platform for innovation, rather than the products or services you sell?

What if you thought in terms of the things you do that other companies cannot?

(*continued*)

(*continued*)

What if you became a platform?

*Reverse*

What if you did more with less?

What if you shifted resources to where the growth potential is?

What if you considered the 80/20 ratio (80 percent performance, 20 percent price)?

*Sustainability*

What if you considered corporate social responsibility not as a philanthropic initiative, but as a way to reinforce your core business?

What if your business became a part of the local community—in every one of your countries?

*Revival*

What if you re-looked at all your abandoned projects in the context of today?

What if a product from the past acquired a different, symbolic value in today's world?

What if you made proprietary technology available to all on Creative Commons?

*Data*

What if you endlessly strived to transform your data into smart data?

What if on top of your core activity, you became a data supplier?

What if you built your customer relations on a related-purchases scheme like Amazon?

*Usage*

What if your online activities dictated your offline offering?

What if you let unexpected usage of your products inspire new product design?

What if you understood better how people relate to your products through their connected devices?

*Price*

What if you decided to offer part of your products and services for free?

What if you "unbundled" the products you sell and only kept what is essential?

What if you added a time limit to your product offering?

*Service*

What if you added services to the physical products you sell?

What if you embodied the services you offer in a physical product?

*Partnership*

What if you partnered with a business as far removed from your own as possible?

What if you linked up with a company operating in the same sector as you?

(*continued*)

*(continued)*

*Brand*

What if your company had a larger purpose than selling?

What if you chose a brand idea strong enough to foster innovation?

What if you started a bonus scheme to reward your employees' innovation ideas throughout the company?

*Insight*

What if you took clusterization all the way to individualization?

What if you created a specific team to turn facts into knowledge and knowledge into insights?

What if you considered doing just the opposite of what strategy consultants usually recommend?

*Business Model*

What if you sold a totally integrated ecosystem?

What if you created a peer-to-peer platform?

What if you transformed one-off sales into long-term subscriptions?

What if you had to face Google as a competitor?

*Anticipation*

What if you decided to innovate in health, education and energy?

What if you deliberately affixed an out-of-reach goal to your company?

# Exhibits

## Exhibit 1: The Disruption Symbols

CONVENTION        DISRUPTION°        VISION

# Exhibit 2: What Makes A Good What If?

The quality of a What If question depends on two criteria, the second being the inverse complement of the first.

To the question: could the What If be imagined without knowing the case? The answer should be no, otherwise the question is not specific enough.

To the question: can you understand the What If, and its relevance, without knowing the case? The answer should be yes, otherwise, the question is not universal enough.

Simply stated, the case inspires the question, which does not need the case to be understood.

# EXhibit 3:  The Fifteen Paths to Innovation

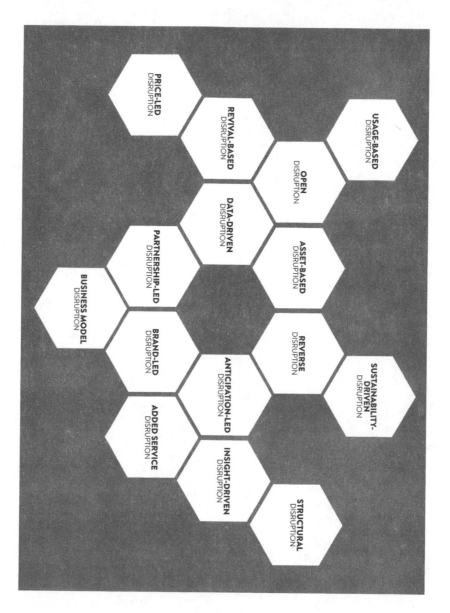

# EXHIBIT 4: TBWA Partners for the Mirai Nihon Project

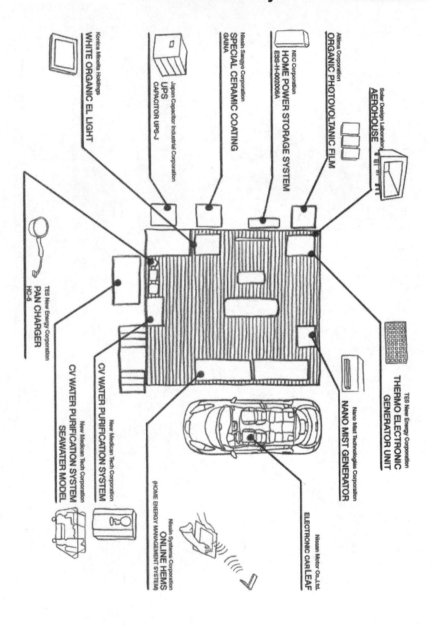

# Exhibit 5: The Mirai Nihon Off-Grid House

# Exhibit 6: The Story of the Disruption Word

On May 12, 1992, we published a full-page advertorial in the *Wall Street Journal* to announce our new strategic approach.

Below the headline, which read simply *Disruption*, a text explained our methodology. Disruption was launched.

## Disruption Before 1992

It all started in Paris, in the 1980s, when many of our clients or prospects assigned to us one of their brands that was in trouble. This forced us to come up with innovative strategies. The French expression we used to describe our way of thinking was *stratégie de rupture*. And this is how it became our specialty. In a tight spot, even a desperate one, we always came up with a daring, risky response. This was a way of going deeper and further into the old idea of breakthrough.

Late in 1990, the strategic planning director of the agency we had just acquired in New York, asked what we meant by *stratégie de rupture*. She liked the approach, but the word *rupture* was obviously a stumbling block. It doesn't work in English. So she came up with some possible terms, among which was the word *disruption*. Until that time, the word was used exclusively in a very negative sense. It was employed to describe something that was problematic or even calamitous, like an earthquake or an epidemic. This is why at the outset, no one was using it in the business community.

Despite the unpleasant connotations, I decided to go ahead with it.

A concept was born. In the beginning, everyone said that we had chosen a very clumsy word. And many were skeptical. I will always remember how uncomfortable, really uncomfortable, many of our clients were with the word when we introduced it in the marketing world. I know for people who are younger than 40 or 50 years old it is difficult to believe, but it was really the case.

Despite the first difficult years, our new method gradually established itself. Disruption took off. And in 1996, we published a book, the first business book in which the word *disruption* was used in a positive way.

## Disruption After 1996

Today, the word has many definitions. In fact, its meaning keeps changing from one day to the next. Business people use it to talk about everything and its opposite; to the point that last year, *The New Yorker* titled an issue: "Disruption has become the norm."

We felt concerned, at the very least, because Disruption is at the core of everything we do at TBWA. And in all our documents, we use the registration symbol, underlining that Disruption is a proprietary process. We own trademark registrations for the Disruption brand across the globe including the United States as well as a large number of countries in Europe, Asia, and Latin America.

So the question is: how come that the definition of a concept, that we created and trademarked, has been distorted so much that some observers and journalists even ended up recommending not to use the word *disruption* anymore. They say they are tired of it.

This needs some explanation.

Some time after our Disruption book came out, Clayton Christensen published, in 1997, *The Innovator's Dilemma* (Harvard Business School Press), which was a huge success. He first talked about what he called disruptive technology, and then more broadly about disruptive innovation. His concept has become an academic theory that serves as a basis for business analysis.

A little bit later, in 1999, Francis Fukuyama published *The Great Disruption* (Reed Business Information). He was the first writer in the business world, after TBWA, to use the noun *"disruption"* and not only the adjective *"disruptive."* But with yet a different meaning. His book dealt with the switch from the industrial era to the information era, which he referred to as "the great disruption."

Then came the Internet. It gave a greater reach to Christensen's definition of disruptive innovation, which became widely accepted. Digital companies brought full force to his concept. It was at that time that on the back cover of one of my books, Tom Peters exclaimed: "Disrupt or be disrupted."

The word *disruption* started being widely used. Start-ups designed and adopted new disruptive business models. The *TechCrunch Disrupt* event was launched. Dozens of articles in magazines such as the *Harvard Business Review* discussed disruptive strategies and benefits derived from Disruption. *Forbes* published an annual list of disruptors, *Bloomberg Businessweek* elected the "Disruptors of the Decade" and *Fortune* even called Steve Jobs the "Master of Disruption."

And it continues. Recently, *The Economist* has organized a seminar in Hong Kong on Disruption. Books have been published with titles such as *Digital Disruption*, *Disruption Revolution*, *Creative Disruption*. Accenture has published *Big Bang Disruption* (Portfolio 2014), a very inspiring essay. These books describe the way many industries such as travel, banking, bookselling, music, retail, telecom, telephone, and automotive have been transformed from top to bottom, mainly by digital.

Most often, business analysts use the word *disruption* to refer to start-ups, especially to those that turn markets upside down. Except for McKinsey, which released a book in May 2015 on the major disruptive trends in health, energy, and education called

*No Ordinary Disruption* (Gildan Media, LLC). The word has yet another meaning, closer to Fukuyama's.

As I already said, we are concerned, not so much because we can claim to have been the first to use the word, which is not so important, but because we do not want something at the core of our culture to become overly used in distorted and misleading ways.

When it comes to defining Disruption from an academic perspective, we recommend not using the definition that refers to start-ups. It is too narrow. And neither McKinsey's, nor Fukuyama's, their definition is too wide.

For us, there is Disruption each time people do not think in a gradual, incremental, linear way. Each time they make strategic leaps. And this can happen at any level. You can imagine a disruptive product, a disruptive business model, a disruptive marketing plan, a disruptive communications strategy.

Bearing this in mind, we have invigorated our 25-year-old concept. It is as relevant today as it was yesterday.

# Acknowledgments

I would like to thank Pamela Tamby, my assistant, for the tremendous work she has done, regarding both the content and the writing of the book. This book would never have existed without her.

I also express my gratitude to Émilie Rousset who stood with me for months and provided me with documentation. She gave this book its initial momentum.

I was fortunate to be surrounded by Pierre Hodgson and Emmanuel de Saint-Martin, two gifted men of letters. I thank both of them for the quality of their work and for their enlightened advice.

I would like to especially thank Guillaume Pannaud for encouraging me to write this book; Nicolas Bordas and Vincent Garel for their input; and Emmanuel André for his insights.

My appreciation goes to Nick Barham, Franck Besson, Djazia Boukhelif, Professor Bernard Charpentier, Fiona Clancy, Bert Denis, Pascal Dupont, Luke Eid, Fabien Gille, Shelby Hutchison, Charlotte Landes, Elizabeth Livio, Miguel Mantilla, Takamatsu Mitsuru, Juuso Myllyrinne, Jean-Marie Prénaud, Jean-François Reiser, Guillaume Schoos, and Jean-David Sichel.

I would like to thank my long-time friend, Nick Baum, for his invaluable contribution and for his unwavering support.

I would also like to thank our CEO, Troy Ruhanen, who by re-insisting on how strategic Disruption is for our network, has given this book its reason for being.

Last, but not least, I would like to thank Richard Narramore, my editor at John Wiley & Sons, for his advice on the overall structure of the book, and his colleagues—Tiffany Colón, Lauren Freestone, Monica James, and Peter Knox—for their precious help in preparing the book and its launch.

# References

## Introduction

1. Drucker, Peter (1954). *The Practice of Management*. New York: Harper & Brothers.

## Chapter One Disruption and the Innovation Deficit

1. Lafley, A.G., and Charan, Ram (2008). *The Game-Changer: How You can Drive Revenue and Profit Growth with Innovation*. New York: Crown Business Publishing.
2. "The Global Innovation 1000 Study." Booz & Company Annual Report (2011).
3. Johansson, Frans (2006). *The Medici Effect. What Elephants and Epidemics Can Teach Us About Innovation*. Boston, Massachusetts: Harvard Business School Press, p.96.

## Chapter Three Disruption in Practice

1. Stone, Brad (May 22, 2013). "Inside Google's Secret Lab." *Bloomberg Businessweek*.
2. Berger, Warren (2014). *A More Beautiful Question: The Power of Inquiry to Spark Breakthrough Ideas*. New York: Bloomsbury, p. 8.

# Chapter Four Open Disruption

1. Huston, Larry and Sakkab, Nabil (March 2006). "Connect and Develop: Inside Procter & Gamble's New Model for Innovation." *Harvard Business Review* 84(03).

2. http://en.wikipedia.org/wiki/Crowdsourcing (accessed August 27, 2015).

3. Lafley, A.G., and Charan, Ram (2008). *The Game-Changer: How You can Drive Revenue and Profit Growth with Innovation.* New York: Crown Business Publishing, p. 132.

4. Lafley, A.G., and Charan, Ram. Op.cit., p. 130.

5. Brown, Bruce and Anthony, Scott (June 2011). "How P&G Tripled its Innovation Success Rate." *Harvard Business Review.*

6. "A.G. Lafley discussing open innovation," 2010 Edison Awards. Available at https://www.youtube.com/watch?v=_7mMToRlAxs (accessed August 27, 2015).

7. Anderson, Chris (2006). *The Long Tail: Why the Future of Business Is Selling Less or More.* New York: Hyperion.

# Chapter Five Structural Disruption

1. Johansson, Frans. Op.cit., p. 79.

2. *PR Newswire UK* (www.prnewswire.co.uk, April 23, 2003). "Nissan annonce une rentabilité record pour l'exercice 2002, avec une marge opérationnelle de 10,8%."

3. Ghosn, Carlos (2004). *Shift: Inside Nissan's Historic Revival.* New York: Crown Business Publishing.

4. Stone, Brad (May 22, 2013). "Inside Google's Secret Lab." *Bloomberg Businessweek.*

5. Dugan, Regina and Gabriel, Kaigham (October 2013). "'Special Forces' Innovation: How DARPA Attacks Problems." *Harvard Business Review*, 91 (10), pp. 74–82.

6. Ibid., p. 76.

7. Ibid.

8. Shah, Semil (www.techcrunch.com, December 4, 2011). "Exploring the "Labs" Trend in Consumer Startups."

9. Dyer, Jeff, Gregersen, Hal B., and Christensen, Clayton M. (2011). *The Innovator's DNA: Mastering the Five Skills of Disruptive Innovators.* Cambridge, MA: Harvard Business Review Press.

10. Rao, Leena (www.techcrunch.com, November 18, 2009). "Salesforce Chatter: A Real-Time Social Network for the Enterprise."

11. *Forbes* (August 13, 2014). "The World's Most Innovative Companies" edition. Available at http://www.forbes.com/innovative-companies/

12. "The Customer Successs Platform: Toyota's vision sets the wheels of society in motion." Available at http://www.salesforce.com/customers/stories/toyota.jsp

13. Anderson, Chris (2012). *Makers: The New Industrial Revolution.* New York: Crown Business Publishing.

14. Ibid., p. 31.

15. Ibid., p. 86.

16. http://www.fabfoundation.org/fab-labs/what-is-a-fab-lab/

17. http://fr.wikipedia.org/wiki/Fab_lab (accessed August 26, 2015).

18. Maker Faire Bay Area 2012. "TechShop Democratizing Access to the Tools of Innovation." Video available at http://library.fora.tv/2012/05/19/TechShop_Democratizing_Access_To_The_Tools_of_Innovation

19. TechShop Press Release (www.techshop.ws, May 4, 2012). "Ford Drives Innovation, Intellectual Property Development through TechShop Membership Incentive for Smart Ideas."

20. http://www.fabfoundation.org/fab-labs/ (accessed August 27, 2015).

21. U.S. Government News Release (www.dol.gov, May 29, 2012). "Obama administration launches $26 million multi-agency competition to strengthen advanced manufacturing clusters across the nation."

22. Anderson, Chris. Op.cit.

23. Ries, Eric (2011). *The Lean Startup: How Today's Entrepreneurs Use Continuous Innovation to Create Radically Successful Businesses.* New York: Crown Business Publishing.

24. Ries, Eric. Op.cit

25. Woo, Ben (*Forbes*, February 14, 2013). "'Innovation Distinguishes Between a Leader and a Follower.'"

# Chapter Six Asset-Based Disruption

1. The Schumpeter Blog (www.economist.com, October 19, 2012). "An A–Z of business quotations: Strategy."

2. Chesbrough, Henry William (2005). *Open Innovation: The New Imperative for Creating and Profiting from Technology.* Cambridge, MA: Harvard Business School Press, p. 163.

3. Chesbrough, Henry William. Op.cit., p. 164.

4. http://www.mentorbit.com/q/291 (accessed August 27, 2015).

5. Zenger, Todd (June 2013). "What Is the Theory of Your Firm?" *Harvard Business Review* 91(6), pp. 73–78.

6. Ibid., p. 75.

7. http://thechallenge.dupont.com/essay/dupont/putting-science-to-work.php (accessed August 27, 2015).

8. https://en.wikipedia.org/wiki/DuPont (accessed August 27, 2015).

9. Walker, Rob (*The New York Times*, November 30, 2003). "The Guts of a New Machine."

# Chapter Seven Reverse Disruption

1. Radjou, Navi, Prabhu, Jaideep, and Ahuja, Simone (2013). *L'Innovation Jugaad. Redevenons Ingénieux!* Strasbourg, France, Les Éditions Diateino, p. 7.

2. Ibid., p.10

3. Govindarajan, Vijay and Trimble, Chris (2012). *Reverse Innovation: Create Far From Home, Win Everywher*e. United States, Harvard Business Press, p. 3.

4. Immelt, Jeffrey, Govindarajan, Vijay, and Trimble, Chris (October 2009). "How GE Is Disrupting Itself." *Harvard Business Review* 87(10).

5. Ibid.

# Chapter Eight Sustainability-Driven Disruption

1. Video available at https://www.youtube.com/watch?v=isjyr0pYvYs

2. Dru, Jean Marie (2012). *Jet-Lag. An Adman's View of the World*. Brooklyn, New York: powerHouse Books.

3. Sheth, Jagdish N., Wolfe David B., and Sisodia, Rajendra S (2006). *Firms of Endearment: How World-Class Companies Profit from Passion and Purpose*. Upper Saddle River, New Jersey: Wharton School Publishing.

4. Video available at https://www.youtube.com/watch?v=3w1LcwEoo5s

5. Liter of Light Web site available at http://literoflight.org/

6. Safian, Robert (*Fast Company*, issue 183, March 2014). "Twelve Innovation Lessons for 2014."

7. Roberts, Daniel (*Fortune*, March 11, 2014). "Can TOMS break into the coffee business?"

8. Roberts, Daniel. Op. cit.

9. Roberts, Daniel. Op. cit.

10. Safian, Robert. Op.cit.

## Chapter Nine Revival-Based Disruption

1. The Schumpeter Blog (www.economist.com, June 14, 2014). "Second wind. Some traditional businesses are thriving in an age of disruptive innovation."

2. Downes, Larry and Nunes, Paul (January 2014). *Big Bang Disruption: Strategy in the Age of Devastating Innovation*. New York, Portfolio/The Penguin Group, p. 108

3. Ibid., p. 109.

4. https://www.kickstarter.com/projects/neolucida/neolucida-a-portable-camera-lucida-for-the-21st-ce

## Chapter Ten Data-Driven Disruption

1. *Contagious X*, 2004–2014 special issue, pp. 64–65.

2. Ibid.

3. Siegler, MG (www.techcrunch.com, August 4, 2010). "Eric Schmidt: Every Two Days We Create as Much Information as We Did Up to 2003."

4. Pearson, Travis and Rasmus Wegener (Bain & Company Inc. Report, 2013). "Big Data: The Organizational Challenge."

5. *Contagious X*, 2004–2014 special issue, p. 58.

6. Hirson, Ron (www.forbes.com, March 23, 2015). "Uber: The Big Data Company."

7. Myers, Chris (www.forbes.com, May 13, 2015). "Decoding Uber's Proposed $50B Valuation (and What It Means for You.)"

8. Manyika, James, Chui, Michael, Brown, Brad, Bughin, Jacques, Dobbs, Richard, Roxburgh, Charles, and Hung Byers, Angela. "Big data: The next frontier for innovation, competition, and productivity." McKinsey Global Institute Report, May 2011. Available at http://www.mckinsey.com/insights/business_technology/big_data_the_next_frontier_for_innovation.

## Chapter Eleven Usage-Based Disruption

1. Colvin, Geoff (www.fortune.com, July 15, 2011). "Zhang Ruimin: Management's next icon."

2. Stengel, Jim (www.jimstengel.com, November 13, 2012). "Wisdom from the Oracle of Qingdao."

3. Gluckman, Ron (www.forbes.com. April 25, 2012). "Appliances for Everyone."

4. The *Hindu Business Line* (www.thehindubusinessline.com, November 5, 2004.) "Haier unveils detergent-free washing machine."

5. Stengel, Jim (www.jimstengel.com, November 13, 2012). "Wisdom from the Oracle of Qingdao."

6. "Regional Economic Outlook: Sub-Saharan Africa, sustaining the expansion." (October 2011). The International Monetary Fund, p. 50.

7. Doran, Sophie (www.luxurysociety.com, January 10, 2014). "How Burberry Does Digital."

8. Ibid.

9. Ibid.

10. Ibid.

11. Davis, Scott (www.forbes.com, March 27, 2014). "Burberry's Blurred Lines: The Integrated Customer Experience."

## Chapter Twelve Price-Led Disruption

1. Radjou, Navi, Prabhu, Jaideep, and Ahuja, Simone (2013). *L'Innovation Jugaad. Redevenons Ingénieux!* France, Les Éditions Diateino.

2. Richaud, Nicolas (www.lesechos.fr, June 10, 2015). "Spotify atteint les 20 millions d'abonnés payants et se prépare à faire face à Apple."

3. Olanoff, Drew (www.techcrunch.com, March 6, 2013). "ZipDial has turned 400M missed calls into moneymaking connections."

## Chapter Thirteen Added-Service Disruption

1. Video available at https://www.youtube.com/watch?v=ulV5LDwdn8Y

2. https://www.pampers.com/login

3. Campbell, Mikey (www.appleinsider.com, April 25, 2014). "Nike to focus on 'digital sport' software, excited about future Apple collaborations."

4. Fleitour, Gaëlle and de Jaegher, Thibaut (www.usine-digitale.fr, September 23, 2014). "Jean-Paul Agon: 'Google ne peut pas tuer L'Oréal, au contraire!'"

5. De Swaan Arons, Marc, van den Driest, Frank, and Weed, Keith (July-August 2014). "The Ultimate Marketing Machine." *Harvard Business Review* 97(7).

6. Krippendorff, Kaihan (www.fastcompany.com, November 14, 2014). "Four Lessons on Running a Successful Business from Best Buy's CEO. How Best Buy's Hubert Joly Turned Around Three Major Businesses and What You Can Learn from Him."

7. http://www.darty.com/achat/services/contrat_de_confiance/index.html

8. Anderson, Chris (2012). *Makers: The New Industrial Revolution.* New York: Crown Business Publishing.

9. Delaune, J., and Everett, W. (2008). Waste and inefficiency in the U.S. health care system—Clinical care. New England Health Institute. Available at http://www.nehi.net/publications/13-waste-and-inefficiency-in-the-u-s-health-care-system-clinical-care/view

## Chapter Fourteen Partnership-Led Disruption

1. *Contagious X*, 2004–2014 special issue, pp. 120–121.

2. Ibid.

3. Gillette, Felix (www.bloomberg.com, February 5, 2014). "Lego Goes to Hollywood." Retrieved from http://www.bloomberg.com/bw/articles/2014-02-05/lego-movie-toy-brands-minifigs-entrusted-to-warner-bros-filmmakers.

4. Rowan, David (www.wired.co.uk, July 3, 2014). "How Tony Fadell brought a touch of Apple to Google."

5. AirBnB Press Release (www.airbnb.fr, on July 31, 2014). "New Study Reveals a Greener Way to Travel: Airbnb Community Shows Environmental Benefits of Home Sharing."

6. D'onfro, Jillian (www.uk.businessinsider.com, April 29, 2015). "How a quirky 28-year-old plowed through $150 million and almost destroyed his start-up."

7. The Statistics Portal (www.statista.com, August 25, 2015). Available at http://www.statista.com/statistics/220718/number-of-employees-at-general-electric/

8. Quirky+Ge Web site available at https://www.quirky.com/ge

9. Mompó, Fernando L. (www.co-society.com, March 15, 2014). "A partnership that will change invention forever."

10. GE Press Release (www.genewsroom.com, November 11, 2014). "Quirky + GE Reveal Blueprint for the Connected Home."

11. BloombergBusiness, The Design Issue (March 20, 2014). "Quirky's Ben Kaufman Gets GE to Share Its Patents."

## Chapter Fifteen Brand-Led Disruption

1. Gallo, Carmine (www.forbes.com, January 17, 2011). "Steve Jobs: 'People With Passion Can Change The World.'"

2. Dru, Jean-Marie (2007). *How Disruption Brought Disorder. The Story of a Winning Strategy in the World of Advertising*. New York: Palgrave.

3. Adidas press release (www.adidas-group.com, February 5, 2004). "'Impossible is Nothing.' Adidas Launches Global Brand Advertising Campaign."

4. Ramchandani, Naresh (www.theguardian.com, September 4, 2006). "A few words that say so much."

5. Source: http://www.tescoplc.com/index.asp?pageid=282

6. Marriott News Center (www.news.marriott.com, September 9, 2014). "Forbes Lists Marriott as Most Innovative Hotel Company."

7. http://travel-brilliantly.marriott.fr/our-innovations/oculus-get-teleported

8. Wasserman, Todd (www.mashable.com, September 18, 2014). "Marriott Can 'Teleport' You to Hawaii or London via Oculus Rift."

9. Rhodes, Margaret (www.wired.co.uk, September 2, 2014). "Marriott's new tables match up guests with LinkedIn interests."

10. http://en.wikipedia.org/wiki/Zappos

11. Hsieh, Tony (2010). *Delivering Happiness: A Path to Profits, Passion and Purpose*. New York: Business Plus/Hachette Book Group.

12. *Fortune.*"100 Best Companies to Work For." Available at http://archive.fortune.com/magazines/fortune/bestcompanies/2009/snapshots/23.html

13. Silverman, Rachel Emma (www.wsj.com, May 20, 2015). "At Zappos, Banishing the Bosses Brings Confusion."

14. Ibid.

15. Hsieh, Tony (blogs.zappos.com, January 3, 2009). "Your Culture Is Your Brand."

16. Lafley, A.G., and Charan, Ram (2008). *The Game-Changer: How You can Drive Revenue and Profit Growth with Innovation*. New York: Crown Business Publishing, p. 12.

# Chapter Sixteen Insight-Driven Disruption

1. Hurnam, James. "Consumer insights: How to catch a heffalump." Master Class at CAANZ/AUT Communications School, 2014.

2. The Library. "2010: Sainsbury's, Marketing Communication–Case Study." Available at https://www.marketingsociety.com/the-library/2010-sainsbury's-marketing-communications-case-study

3. Hurnam, James (www.newretailblog.com, October 10, 2012). "Insights from the shop floor."

4. Ibid.

5. Hurnam, James. "Consumer insights: How to catch a heffalump." Master Class at CAANZ/AUT Communications School, 2014.

6. Procter & Gamble's Internal Memo.

7. Lafley, A.G., and Charan, Ram (2008). *The Game-Changer: How You can Drive Revenue and Profit Growth with Innovation*. New York: Crown Business Publishing.

8. L'Oréal website. Research & Innovation homepage available at http://www.loreal.com/research-and-innovation

9. "Laurent Attal: Doctor of the Universe." Retrieved from L'Oréal's U.S.A. blog (lorealusablog.wordpress.com, October, 14 2013).

10. Big Bazaar Web site available http://bigbazaarfranchisee.com/about-us

11. "Big Bazaar opens its store at Agartala on 10th July, 2013." Retrieved from www.tripuramirror.com.

12. https://en.wikipedia.org/wiki/Big_Bazaar (accessed on August 27, 2015).

13. Biyani, Kishore and Baishya, Dipayan (2007). *It happened in India: The Story of Pantaloons, Big Bazaar, Central and the Great Indian Consumer.* New Delhi: Rupa Publications India Pvt. Ltd.

14. Big Bazaar Web site available at http://bigbazaarfranchisee.com/about-us

15. Interview of Kishore Biyani with India Knowledge@Wharton. "Retailer Kishore Biyani: 'We Believe in Destroying What We Have Created." Retrieved from knowledge.wharton.upenn.edu, November 1, 2007.

16. Bulygo, Zach (blog.kissmetrics.com, September 6, 2013). "How Netflix Uses Analytics to Select Movies, Create Content, and Make Multimillion Dollar Decisions."

17. Laporte, Nicole (www.fastcompany.com, April 7, 2015). "HBO to Netflix: Bring It On: How HBO's quest to win the streaming wars became a binge-worthy drama as juicy as *Game of Thrones.*"

18. Carr, David (www.nytimes.com, February 24, 2013). "Giving Viewers What They Want."

# Chapter Seventeen Business Model Innovation

1. De Foucaud, Isabelle (www.lefigaro.fr, January 13, 2015). "Conso malin: J'ouvre un compte bancaire au bureau de tabac pour 20 euros."

2. Renaud, Ninon (www.lesechos.fr, January 13, 2015). "Le compte Nickel vise 220.000 clients en 2015."

3. Ibid.

4. Chesbrough, Henry William (2011). *Open Services Innovation: Rethinking Your Business to Grow and Compete in a New Era.* San Francisco, CA: Jossey-Bass/A Wiley Imprint, p. 105.

5. Ibid., p.107.

6. Facebook Newsroom Page available at http://newsroom.fb.com/company-info

7. *Contagious X*, 2004–2014 special issue, pp. 24–25

8. "The Missing Piece." Tesla Powerfull Keynote by Elon Musk in Los Angeles on April 30, 2015. Available at https://www.youtube.com/watch?v=yKORsrlN-2k

9. Ibid.

10. Kopytoff, Verne (www.fortune.com, May 6, 2014). "Jack Ma, Alibaba's founder, in the IPO spotlight."

11. Alibaba Group Company Overview. Available at: http://www.alibabagroup.com/en/about/overview.

12. Wong, Gillian, Chu, Kathy, and Osawa, Juro (www.wsj.com, March 2, 2015). "Inside Alibaba, the Sharp-Elbowed World of Chinese E-Commerce."

13. Winkler, Matthew, Yamaguchi, Yuki, and Teo, Chian-Wei (www.bloomberg.com, October 12, 2012). "Rakuten Seeks Asia Growth as Japan Online Mall Chases Amazon."

14. Erickson, Jim (www.alizila.com, January 23, 2015). "Jack Ma at Davos: 'We Can Serve 2 Billion Consumers.'"

15. Ibid.

16. Indvik, Lauren (www.mashable.com, May 20, 2012). "E-commerce in China: How the World's Biggest Market Buys Online."

17. O'Connor, Clare (www.forbes.com, November 11, 2014). "Macy's, Saks, Bloomingdale's and More Accept Alipay to Woo Rich Chinese Shoppers."

18. Wang, Helen H, (www.forbes.com, August 7, 2014). "Alibaba Saga IV: A Crocodile In The Yangtze River."

19. Zeng, Vanessa, Wang, Bryan, Barnes, Michael, and Jin, Di (Forrester Research Inc. Report, February 2015). "China Online Retail Forecast, 2014 to 2019. Embrace the Mobiles Sales Momentum in China."

# Chapter Eighteen Anticipation-Driven Disruption

1. "Mirai Nihon Project. A project to design a 100% off-grid lifestyle for Japan's future." Available at http://www.tbwahakuhodo.co.jp/mirainihon/

2. Quote retrieved from Mirai Nihon Project video. Available at https://vimeo.com/43008478

3. "Can Google Solve Death?" *Time* magazine cover retrieved from *Time* website (September 30, 2013). Available at http://content.time.com/time/covers/0,16641,20130930,00.html

4. Apple Distinguished Educators Web site available at http://www.apple.com/education/apple-distinguished-educator/

5. Bloem, Jaap (labs.sogeti.com, May 1, 2014). "IBM's Smarter Cities Challenge: A 5-Year Evaluation."

6. "World Urbanization Prospects: The 2014 Revision, Highlights." Report of the U.N. Department of Economic and Social Affairs. New York: United Nations, 2014. Available at http://www.un.org/en/globalissues/humansettlements/

## Chapter Twenty Disruption Live

1. NURVE platform available at http://r3integration40.com/project/nurve-nissan-united-real-time-vision-for-engagement/

## Conclusion

1. Taylor, William C., and Labarre, Polly (2006). *Mavericks at Work: Why the Most Original Minds in Business Win.* New York: William Morrow/HarperCollins Publishers.
2. Richmond, Shane (www.telegraph.co.uk, May 23, 2012). "Jonathan Ive interview: Simplicity isn't simple."

# Bibliography

Anderson, Chris. *The Long Tail: Why the Future of Business Is Selling Less or More*. New York: Hyperion, 2006.

Anderson, Chris. *Makers: The New Industrial Revolution*. New York: Crown Business, 2012.

Berger, Warren. *A More Beautiful Question: The Power of Inquiry to Spark Breakthrough Ideas*. New York: Bloomsbury, 2014.

Chesbrough, Henry William. *Open Innovation: The New Imperative for Creating and Profiting from Technology*. Cambridge, MA: Harvard Business School Press, 2005.

Chesbrough, Henry William. *Open Services Innovation: Rethinking Your Business to Grow and Compete in a New Era*. San Francisco, CA: Jossey-Bass/A Wiley Imprint, 2011.

Downes, Larry, and Nunes, Paul. *Big Bang Disruption: Strategy in the Age of Devastating Innovation*. New York: Penguin Group, 2014.

Dru, Jean-Marie. *How Disruption Brought Order: The Story of a Winning Strategy in the World of Advertising*. New York: Palgrave Macmillan, 2007.

Dru, Jean-Marie. *Jet-Lag. An Adman's View of the World*. Brooklyn, NY: powerHouse Books, 2012.

Drucker, Peter. *The Practice of Management*. New York: Harper & Brothers, 1954.

Dyer, Jeffrey H., Gregersen, Hal B., and Christensen, Clayton M. *The Innovator's DNA: Mastering the Five Skills of Disruptive Innovators*. Cambridge, MA: Harvard Business Review Press, 2011.

Ghosn, Carlos. *Shift: Inside Nissan's Historic Revival*. New York: Crown Business Publishing, 2004.

Govindarajan, Vijay, and Trimble, Chris. *Reverse Innovation: Create Far From Home, Win Everywhere*. Cambridge, MA: Harvard Business Review Press, 2012.

Hsieh, Tony. *Delivering Happiness: A Path to Profits, Passion and Purpose*. New York: Business Plus/Hachette, 2010.

Johansson, Frans. *The Medici Effect: What Elephants and Epidemics Can Teach Us About Innovation*. Boston, MA: Harvard Business School Press, 2006.

Keely, Larry, Pikkel, Ryan, Quinn, Brian, and Walters, Helen. *Ten Types of Innovation. The discipline of Building Breakthroughs*. Hoboken, New Jersey: Wiley & Sons Inc., 2013.

Lafley, A.G., and Charan, Ram. *The Game-Changer: How You can Drive Revenue and Profit Growth with Innovation*. New York: Crown Business Publishing, 2008.

Moore, Geoffrey A. *Dealing With Darwin: How Great Companies Innovate at Every Phase of Their Evolution*. New York: Penguin Group, 2008.

Morris, Langdon, Ma, Moses, and Wu, Po Chi. *Agile Innovation: The Revolutionary Approach to Accelerate Success, Inspire Engagement and Ignite Creativity*. Hoboken, New Jersey: Wiley & Sons, Inc., 2014.

Passiak, David. *Disruption Revolution. Innovation, Entrepreneurship, and the New Rules of Leadership*. Brooklyn, New York: Social Mediate Press, 2013.

Radjou, Navi, Prabhu, Jaideep, and Ahuja, Simone. *Jugaad Innovation: Think Frugal, Be Flexible, Generate Breakthrough Growth*. New York: Jossey-Bass, A Wiley Imprint, 2013.

Radjou, Navi, and Prabhu, Jaideep. *L'innovation frugale. Comment faire mieux avec moins*. Strasbourg: Les Éditions Diaeino, 2015.

Sheth, Jagdish N., Wolfe, David B., and Sisodia, Rajendra S. *Firms of Endearment: How World-Class Companies Profit from Passion and Purpose*. Upper Saddle River, NJ: Pearson Prentice Hall, 2006.

Taylor, William C., and Labarre Polly. *Mavericks at Work: Why the Most Original Minds in Business Win*. New York: William Morrow/HarperCollins Publishers, 2006.

# Index

Note: Page references in *italics* refer to exhibits.